More Needlepoint from America's Great Quilt Designs

More Needlepoint from America's Great Quilt Designs

Mary Kay Davis and Helen Giammattei

Illustrated by Elizabeth Meyer

Photographed by Mason Pawlak of
Boulevard Photographic, Inc.

WD

WORKMAN PUBLISHING COMPANY, NEW YORK

Published simultaneously in Canada
by Saunders of Toronto, Inc.

Library of Congress Cataloging in Publication Data

Davis, Mary Kay.
More needlepoint from America's great quilt designs.

Bibliography: p.
1. Canvas embroidery—Patterns. 2. Coverlets,
American. I. Giammattei, Helen, joint author.
II. Title.
TT778.C3D39   1977   746.4'4   77-5305
ISBN 0-89480-005-1
ISBN 0-89480-006-X pbk.

Workman Publishing Company
231 East 51 Street
New York, New York 10022

Jacket design by Paul Hanson
Illustrations by Elizabeth Meyer
Photographs by Mason Pawlak
Yarn by Appleton Brothers, Ltd.
Manufactured in the United States of America

First printing November 1977
10 9 8 7 6 5 4 3 2 1

To
Katherine Wagner,
Mary Kay's mother
and
Pres, Bruce, and Jane Giammattei,
Helen's children

Acknowledgments

The thank-you list grows longer the second time around! Our hearts and thanks go to our husbands, Mike Davis and Frank Giammattei, for bearing with us through another book.

We had the help of expert and dedicated stitchers. Our warmest thanks go to Durinda Brownlee, Patricia Burns, Bunny Ebeling, Sunny Erwin, Jane Giammattei, Sally Henby, Mary K. Larson, Jean McCue, Carolyn Moore, Susan Reepmeyer, Deborah Sloan, and Betsy Taylor.

The library staff of the Henry Ford Museum provided unfailing help during the research process. Our thanks also go to Dick Crandall of Boulevard Photographic, Inc., and to Marsha Mettler for her truly expert finishing.

We are grateful to Elva Adams of the Warren County Historical Society for introducing us to a scrapbook of early twentieth-century quilt patterns compiled by the late Mrs. Mary Michener. Some of our needlepoint patterns are based on this scrapbook, and we are particularly grateful to its owner, Mrs. Richard Rosell, for allowing us access to it.

Contents

Preface

Throughout all of American and most of European history, a distinction has been made between what were termed the *fine arts* and the *decorative arts.* Fine arts included painting and sculpture. Decorative arts encompassed such crafts as embroidery, pottery, and wood carving.

Fine arts have always been greatly prized, for they delight the eyes. But they cannot keep you warm, attract mallards, or hold soup. Therefore, painting and sculpture fit the definition of a luxury: "Anything which pleases the senses, and is also costly."

The decorative arts stem from a desire to make what you need look more attractive. With few exceptions, they were used until they wore out; and because the item was necessary whether or not it was decorated, the addition of decoration usually added little to its value.

The fine artists of history were, with few exceptions, men. The decorative artists were of both sexes. Men usually excelled at the crafts that required strength, such as furniture making and glassblowing. Women stayed nearer home, and their decorative artistry appeared in the textile arts of embroidery and quilt making.

In early America, there was little time or money for luxuries or the fine arts. Lines of responsibility were firmly drawn within the family. Men provided housing, protection, and food, which they obtained by farming, hunting, or trading. Women kept the house, raised the children, fed everyone, and were in charge of producing cloth and clothing for the family and the home.

America's pioneer women spent most of their lives coping with dirt, food, gardens, and children. Quilting and embroidery were important artistic outlets for them because, unlike those other occupations, needlework was a lasting accomplishment that could be viewed with pride long after the labor was finished. No wonder these textiles were stitched with such pleasure and kept with such pride.

But quilts, coverlets, and samplers were never thought of as objects of art. They were first and foremost functional items that would make life a little more comfortable. If they could be made attractive, so much the better. The housewife at her fireside never conceived of her handwork as an art form, and yet, in many cases, that is exactly what it was.

Today, we are beginning to value these textiles more for their artistic merit than for their utility. And in doing so, we are moving them from the area of decorative arts to that of the fine arts. How surprised our foremothers would be!

What Every Needleworker Should Know

CANVAS OR CLOTH

- All designs in this book can be worked on needlepoint canvas or on evenweave fabric. However, we feel that open designs with large background areas lend themselves to embroidery on cloth and that solid patterns are better worked on canvas.

- Canvas may be stitched with or without a frame, as you prefer. However, for best results on evenweave cloth, the fabric should be stretched taut. Tack or sew all four edges to a frame or stretcher before you begin stitching.

- *Gauge* is the size of the canvas or evenweave cloth. A #14 canvas has 14 threads per inch and is finer than #8 canvas or cloth that has 8 threads to the inch.

- Leave a minimum of 1½″ unworked canvas or cloth on all four sides. This is necessary for blocking and finishing.

- Mark the canvas as little as possible. Use india ink and a quill pen or a waterproof marking pen that you are certain is waterproof. (See Sampler Introduction, page 160 for testing procedure.)

- Count the threads of the canvas, not the holes. Each stitch covers its own number of threads, but different stitches use the same hole.

YARN

- Anchor the first needlefull of yarn on the back of the canvas by burying its end beneath the first ten stitches. After that, anchor all beginnings and endings of yarn by weaving them through the back of completed stitching.

- To determine how many strands of yarn to use for a particular gauge cloth or canvas, consult the Canvas-Needle-Yarn Chart (page 205).

- A *straight stitch* is one that lies parallel to the threads of the canvas, either horizontally or vertically. Straight stitches usually require one more strand of yarn than diagonal stitches to cover the canvas.

- A *diagonal stitch* is one that lies diagonally across the intersection of canvas threads.

- When a straight stitch meets a diagonal stitch, one must overlap the other so that the canvas does not show. Always allow the pattern stitch to overlap the background stitch.

- Diagonal stitches can pull canvas or cloth out of shape. If the pattern you choose is composed primarily of diagonal stitches in one direction, the piece will keep its shape better if worked on a frame.

STITCHING TECHNIQUES

- Flatten the yarn. Keep strands side by side, like railroad tracks, instead of twisted, like a candy cane. The flattened yarn will cover the canvas better and will produce a more uniform surface.

● Regulate tension so that yarn lies smoothly on the canvas or cloth without pulling the meshes out of shape.

● Whenever possible, bring the needle up in an empty hole and down in a hole that contains yarn. Stitch using two motions except when working the basketweave and long-armed cross stitches.

● When light and dark wools share holes, stray fibers of the dark may be picked up by the light yarn. To prevent this, work light-colored areas first whenever possible.

● Be gentle with the canvas. If you cannot reach the center of your work easily, roll the excess canvas; do not crease, wrinkle or crumple it.

● We rarely turn our canvas as we stitch alternating rows. Work back and forth, leaving your canvas right side up.

USING THIS BOOK

● Stitches that make up each design are generally diagramed in the graph for that particular design. In the few cases where undiagramed stitches are mentioned in a pattern's Stitching Directions, the number following the stitch name refers to its diagram in the Stitching Guide, which begins on page 194.

● Some patterns in the Amish section and all patterns in the Sampler section have an overall diagram in addition to the stitching diagram for each design. In the Amish section, the numbers printed on each section of an overall diagram refer to the number of canvas threads contained within that particular section; in the Sampler section, the numbers refer to the number of the individual stitch diagram in the Stitching Guide.

● Many of the stitching diagrams show only one color. You can check the color photographs of the completed pieces to see where color changes take place.

Designs in Color

The following sixteen pages show each needlepoint design in a full-color photograph. Here the authors, Mary Kay Davis and Helen Ill Giammattei, display their finished work.

1

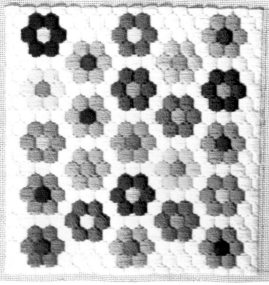

2

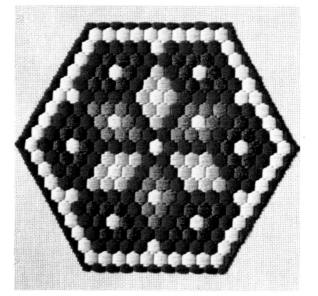

4

3

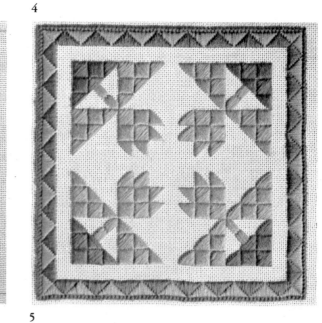

5

1

4

2

5

3

6

1

2

3

4

5

6

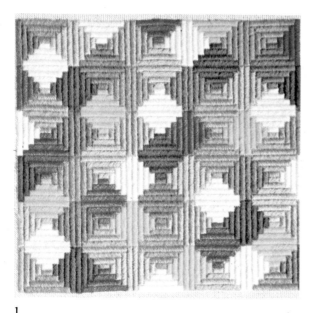

1

3

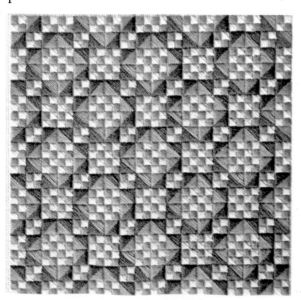

2

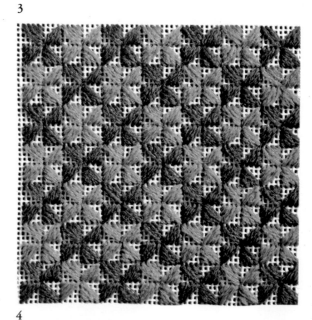

4

1

2

3

4

5

6

Blazing Star, page 74

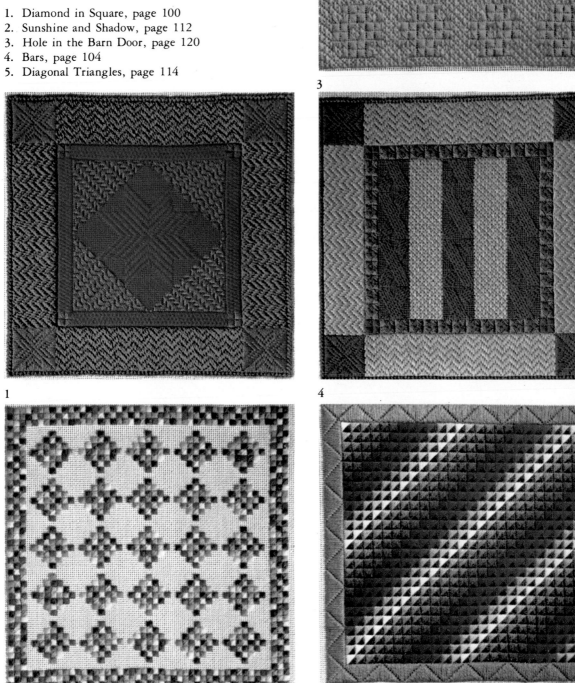

3

1

4

2

5

Roman Stripe, page 116

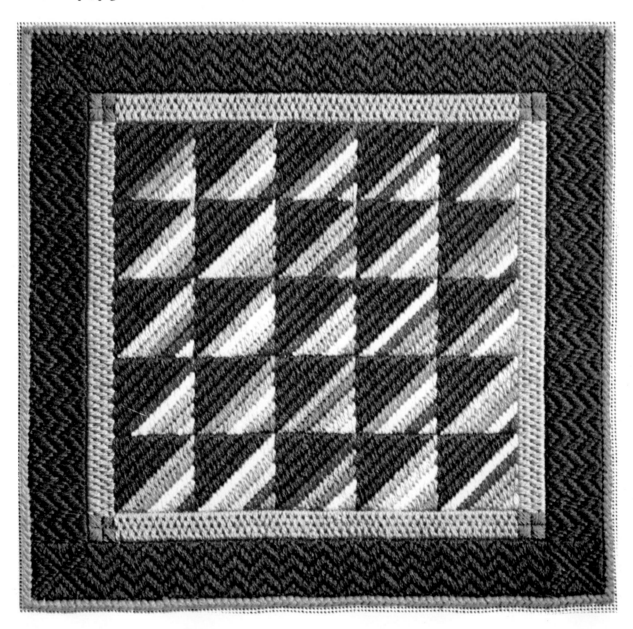

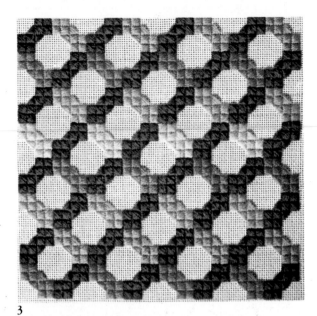

3

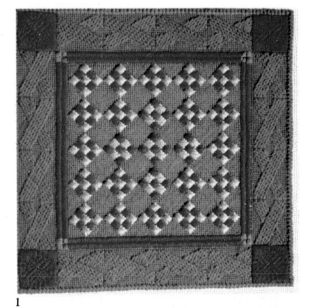

1

4

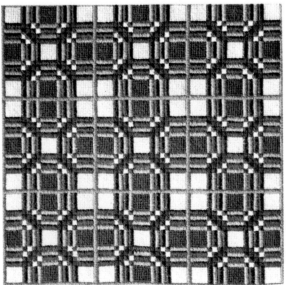

2

5

Village Green, page 142

1

5

9

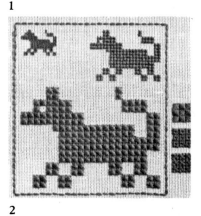

2

6

10

3

7

11

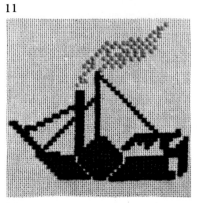

4

8

12

1

2

3

4

5

6

1

3

2

4

Maple Leaf, page 162

Pieced Quilts

When European women first arrived in America, they brought with them a long quilting tradition. Soon the warm quilts filled with wool that were widely used back home in northern Europe were being produced in America, but with a difference. The European quilts were made of two sheets of whole cloth, stuffed and elaborately quilted. Life in the New World was hard, and the American quilts had to be composed of any bits and pieces of cloth that were available. Economy thus produced one of the first truly American art forms: pieced quilts.

These women, who were English and Dutch, made their new homes along the Atlantic coastline from New England south to the Middle Atlantic colonies.

Before the American Revolution, the land available to settlers was limited by English law to a narrow strip between the Atlantic Coast and the Appalachian mountains. But after the United States was established, colonists began moving west. They went through mountain gaps or along rivers and opened up the heart of the continent. The names of the quilts that American women pieced have always reflected what was on their minds. Road to Tennessee and, later, Road to California are patterns that originated during this period of western expansion.

But the frontier was not all these women thought of. Patriotism moved them, and they stitched American Flag quilts. Their homes were on their minds, and patterns such as Broken Dishes reflected everyday concerns. Hole in the Barn Door indicates that house-keeping was as funny and frustrating then as it is now. And their children were always in their thoughts. The quilt pattern known as Whirligig was inspired by a child's toy that operated much as today's pinwheel does.

In the first years of the nineteenth century, women who lived along America's Atlantic Coast stitched such quilts as Ships at Sea and Sailboats. Those who lived inland had other things on their minds. They quilted the Pine Tree, the Pine Cone, and most ominous of all, the Broad Arrow.

But East or West, these women wanted beauty and had little opportunity to achieve it. A woman's garden and her quilts were often the only artistic outlets available to her. So it is not surprising that flower names were often given to quilt designs. Such patterns as Chrysanthemum, Spring Garden, Magnolia, and Grandmother's Flower Garden were favorites.

Before the Civil War, quilt patterns were regional in character. A woman would exchange patterns with her neighbors and might see new designs at local fairs. But she was often unaware of what women fifty miles away were quilting. Names for the same pattern often differed in different areas; consequently, one quilt design may have many aliases.

By 1820, the population of the young nation was growing rapidly. Most women quilted, and many quilting traditions sprang up. The quilting bee was one such institution. Bees were gatherings at which neighbors helped each other with time-consuming or difficult work. Barn raisings and cornhuskings were gatherings of this type, too, but quilting bees were highest on the community's social scale. Attending a quilting bee was rather like going to church; it gave people a chance to get dressed up in their best clothes.

Quilting superstitions abounded. One of the earliest was that there was a hex on the pattern ominously named Wandering Foot. Supposedly, any young man unfortunate enough to sleep beneath a Wandering Foot quilt would head west straightaway, dragging his family willy-nilly behind him. Obviously, this belief limited the number of Wandering Foot quilts pieced. In the middle of the nineteenth century, however, the name was changed to Turkey Tracks, and the jinx mysteriously vanished. Another superstition centered on weddings. Hearts were a popular bridal symbol and were often used in piecing and quilting bride's quilts. But according to the superstition, any girl who had the audacity to stitch hearts before she was firmly engaged would never catch a husband.

All the sewing necessary to clothe a family and furnish a home was done by the women of the house. A girl's education in needlework began early. Tradition declared that a girl have twelve quilt tops stitched and in her bride chest before she married. The tops were made of clothing scraps and cost nothing but time to manufacture, but they were not filled and backed until a son-in-law was in sight because backings and fillings were store goods and cost money. The gatherings at which a bride's quilts were finished were the forerunners of today's engagement parties.

A gifted seamstress might work two quilts simultaneously. Her *masterpiece* was difficult and stitched only in the daytime, when the light was good and she was fresh. The other quilt was called a *utility* and used the scraps left over from the masterpiece. Utility quilts were pickup work for after dark, when the light was poor and the stitcher was tired.

Masterpiece quilts were often composed of diamonds or hexagons consisting of pieces of fabric cut on the bias. These bits of cloth would stretch and pucker if not handled carefully. When well stitched, they bore tribute to the skill of an accomplished needlewoman. The Blazing Star is such a masterpiece pattern. Hexagonal designs include Rainbow Tiles, Hexagon Star, Honeycomb, and Grandmother's Flower Garden.

The Civil War produced few Southern quilt patterns except the Confederate Star. But after the war, customs changed rapidly. Magazines such as *Godey's Lady's Book* were circulated coast to coast and began to feature quilt patterns, making the same patterns available to everyone. Regional designs began to disappear, and soon all Victorian America seemed to be embroidering elaborate crazy quilts and piecing Log Cabin patterns.

Log Cabin quilts were composed of ribbon-shaped strips of cloth sewed together in much the same way that logs were placed to form a cabin. The arrangement of light and dark areas formed many Log Cabin variations that bore such names as Barn Raising and Courthouse Steps.

By America's centennial, its industry could produce blankets inexpensively and in sufficient quantities to supply the whole population. A woman no longer needed to quilt to keep her family warm. So the function of quilts changed. They became objects of decoration, not of necessity. Pictures appeared, such as Flower Baskets and Bow Ties. Today, quilts remain objects of decoration, for we are still enchanted by these hypnotizing patterns.

Honeycomb

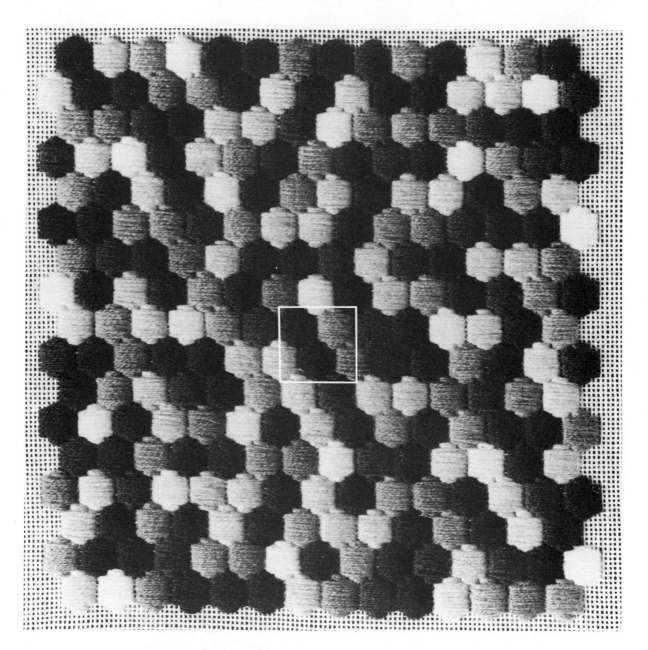

The Honeycomb pattern is an eighteenth-century example of a one-patch quilt. Hexagons were sewed together at random, without any attempt at color arrangement. A seamstress began with one hexagon in the center of what was to be the quilt top and sewed patch to patch until the top was finished. If one hexagon was cut improperly or any of the patches were stretched on the bias, the pattern would seem to be askew, and the puckered quilt would not lie flat. By the time the quilt top had grown to be approxi-

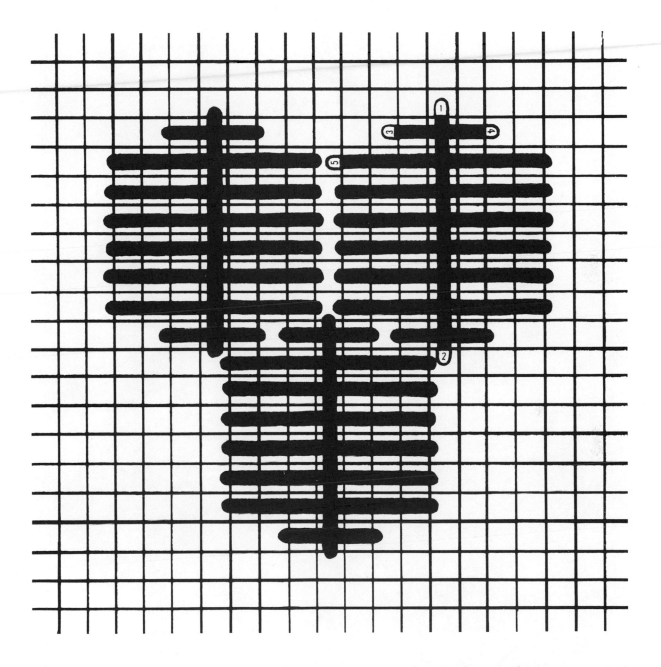

mately 100 inches square, the problem of handling it without stretching must have been immense. No wonder hexagon designs were considered masterpiece quilts.

Stitching Directions. To stitch each hexagon, begin by working 1 vertical stitch over 9 threads as diagramed. Cover this stitch with 8 horizontal stitches as diagramed. Begin the Honeycomb anywhere. It's a wonderful way to use leftover yarn. The finished piece measures 9″ square on #14 canvas.

Hexagon Star

The Hexagon Star is an example of a mosaic quilt, for unlike the Honeycomb pattern, this design attempts to sort and organize colors. Hexagonal patterns lent themselves to intricate designs, and the patterns that resulted ranged from simple to very elaborate.

One-patch mosaic quilts were ex-tremely difficult to work because the stitcher had to envision the entire design in all its complexities before she took one stitch. A few deviations from a complex pattern and the whole design might dissolve into a collection of ran-dom hexagons (a Honeycomb).

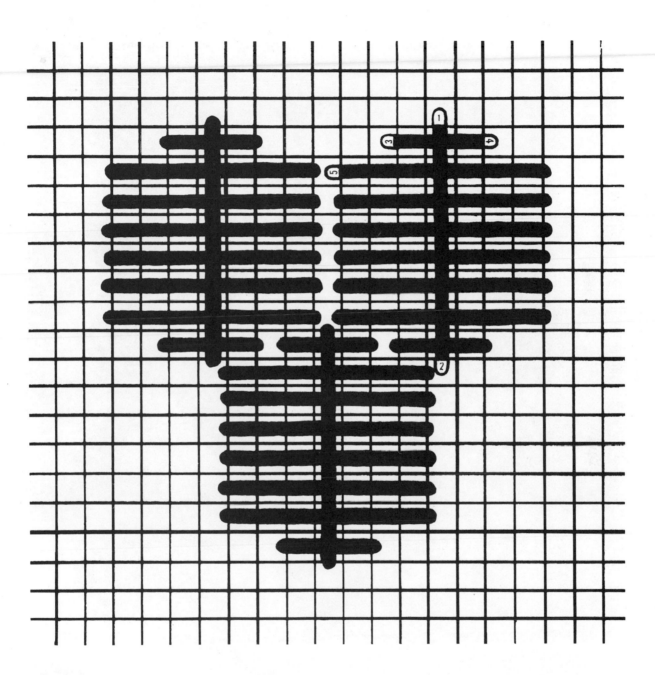

Stitching Directions. Start the Hexagon Star in the center, and work the star in concentric rings, finishing one color before you begin the next. Stitch each hexagon by working 1 vertical stitch over 9 threads as diagramed. Cover this stitch with 8 horizontal stitches as diagramed. Complete the pattern by working the background hexagons. The finished piece measures 14″ square on #14 canvas.

Grandmother's Flower Garden

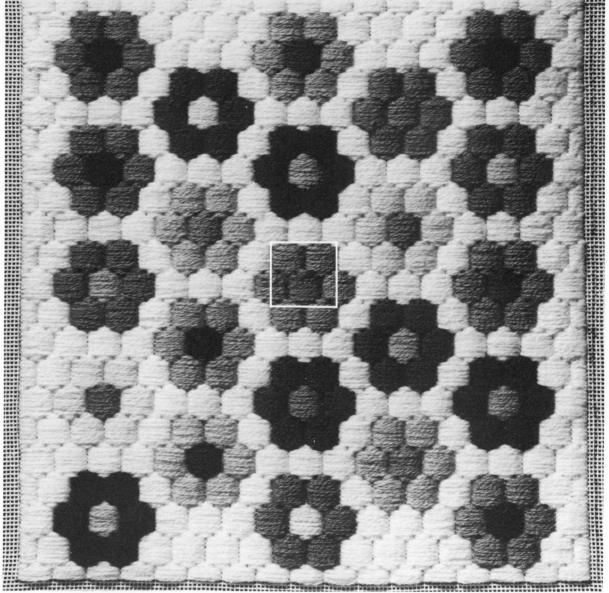

Grandmother's Flower Garden was also called Martha Washington's Bouquet or French Bouquet. It was one of the most popular mosaic patterns of the late eighteenth and early nineteenth centuries. Hexagons were difficult to cut precisely. The size of each hexagon was a matter of pride. The smaller the bits of cloth, the more skillful the sewer. Hexagons sometimes measured less than 1 inch across. One quilt is said to contain over 3,600 individual patches. A well-stitched hexagon quilt was clearly the sign of an accomplished seamstress.

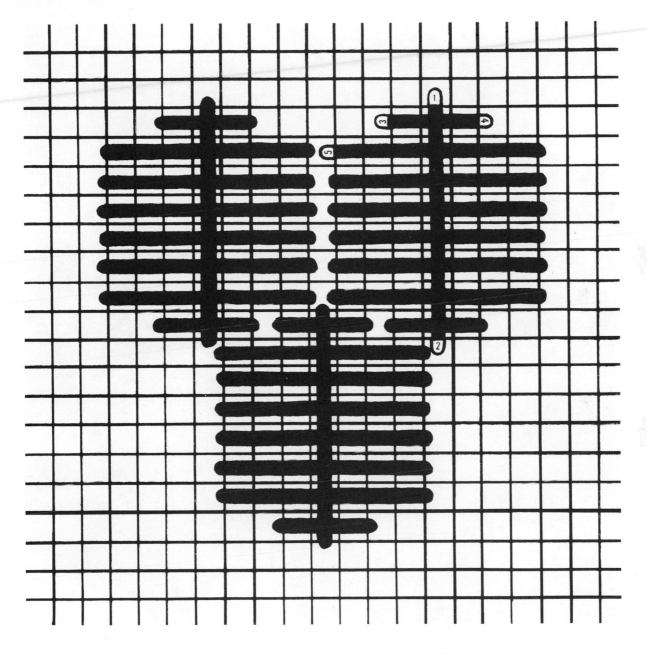

Stitching Directions. To stitch each hexagon, begin by working 1 vertical stitch over 9 threads as diagramed. Cover this stitch with 8 horizontal stitches as diagramed. Stitch the central flower first. Complete the flowers, leaving space between them (see the photograph on the opposite page) for the background hexagons. The finished piece measures 11″ square on #14 canvas.

Rainbow Tiles

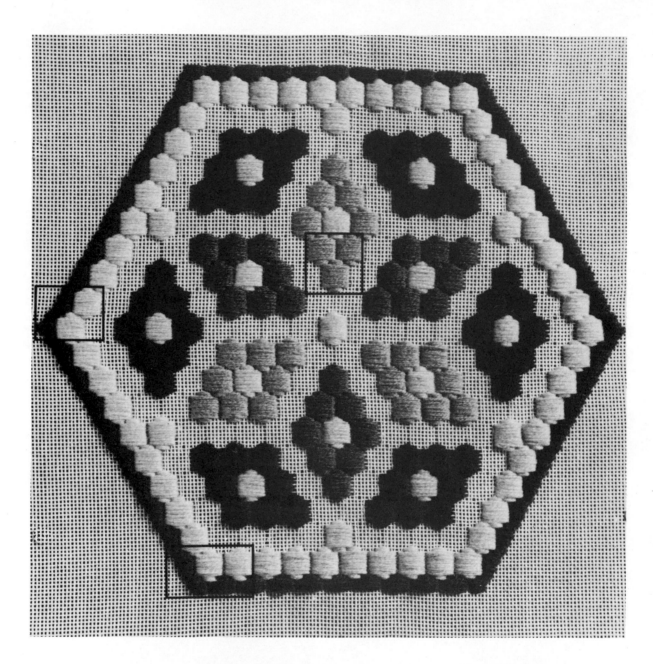

Rainbow Tiles, also called Diamond Field, was a less common mosaic pattern than Grandmother's Flower Garden. One problem with hexagonal designs was that they could not easily fit into the square quilt block on which most nineteenth-century quilts were based. Tiny hexagonal patches produced large hexagonal blocks that, if carried to their ultimate extreme, would have produced huge hexagonal quilts. It all had to end somewhere, and the individual stitcher's solution to this puzzle gives us some of our most exciting mosaic patterns. Rainbow Tiles can give the effect of a stained-glass window in a cathedral.

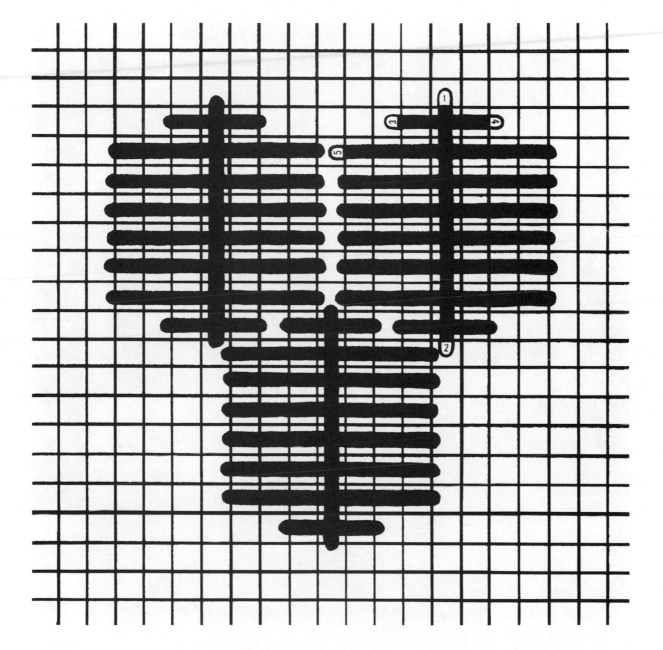

Stitching Directions. To stitch each hexagon, begin by working 1 vertical stitch over 9 threads as diagramed. Cover the vertical stitch with 8 horizontal stitches as diagramed. Begin Rainbow Tiles by working the single hexagon that forms the pattern's center. Stitch the 6 diamonds nearest the center next. Work the 6 outer diamonds last. Fill in the background with hexagons. Complete by smoothing the outer edges with the Rainbow Tiles border as diagramed on page 192. The finished piece measures 11″ × 12″ on #14 canvas.

Spring Garden 1

We have enlarged and used the diagramed tulip patch in two ways to produce two very different designs, as photographed. In the version with the lighter flowers, the pots point inward and the flowers face out. In the version with the darker flowers, these directions are reversed. Such games could be played with other quilt designs, such as Flower Baskets.

Spring Garden 2

A woman would piece a number of identical quilt blocks. Then she would place them on the top of a bed and turn them this way and that, until she had an interesting arrangement. She might separate blocks with a lattice, allow them to touch each other, or divide them with squares or diamonds of plain cloth. Each variation could be, and often was, given a different name.

See detail on page 48.

Spring Garden Detail

Stitching Directions. Begin stitching at the base of the pot, and work upward. Complete the leaves and then the flower as diagramed. Complete the background of the square. The finished piece measures 2″ square on #14 canvas.

The two enlarged Spring Garden variations photographed are stitched in the same sequence and in the same way as the smaller diagramed version.

The canvas size has been enlarged from #14 to #10. Each square now covers 8 threads instead of 4. The

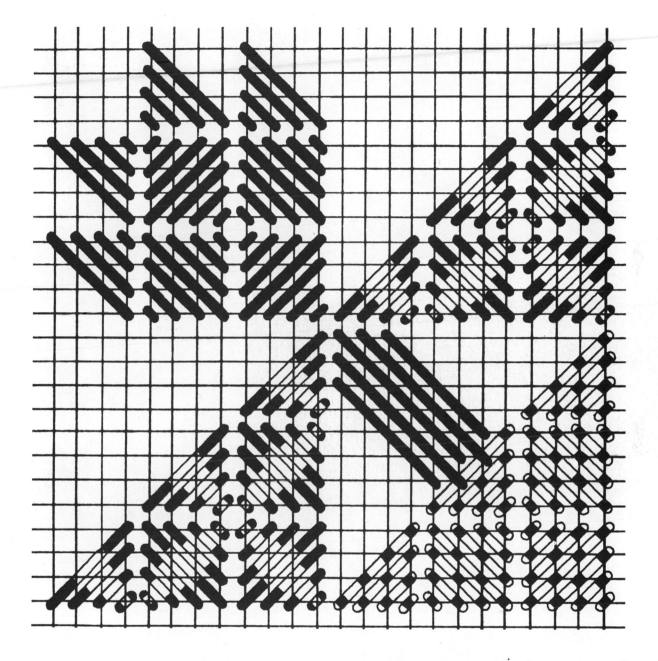

squares are arranged exactly as diagramed, but each covers twice as many threads. To stitch the border, begin at the center of each side. Place dark triangles on either side of the center and work the border toward corners as diagramed on page 189. The recommended background stitch is basketweave.

These finished pieces measure 13″ square on #10 canvas.

Variation: Belts, luggage straps, and bell pulls can be worked with the small diagramed squares. Alternate flower directions so that the pot of one square touches the flower of the next.

Pine Tree

The Pine Tree pattern, with its Pine Cone border, is an excellent example of a quilt design inspired by the untamed land that surrounded settlers' cabins. A pine tree was the symbol of colonial America from its earliest days. When the first mint was established by the British in Massachusetts in 1652, all coins were required to have a "characteristic emblem" stamped on one side. The emblem chosen was the Pine Tree, and pine tree shillings are collectors' items today. Maine is still called the Pine Tree State.

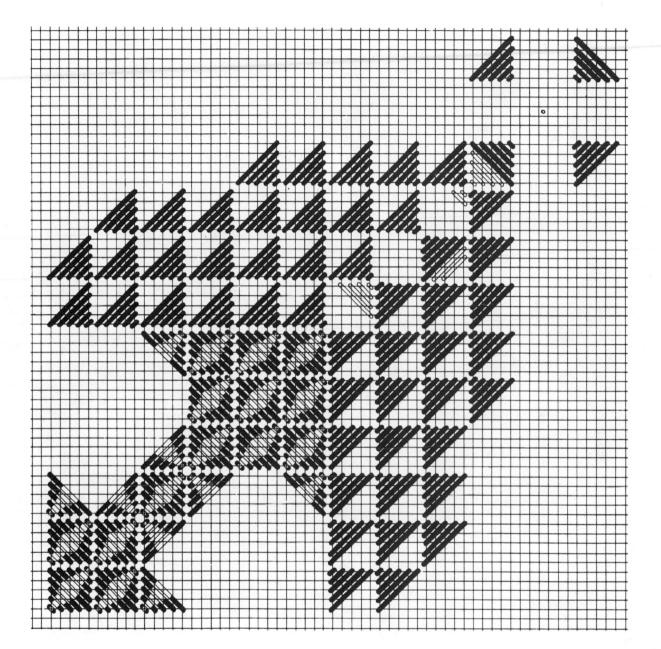

Stitching Directions. Work the Pine Cone border first, as diagramed on page 191. Take careful note of the direction in which each cone points; they change direction in the center of each side. This pattern should be worked on a frame, and it would look equally well on even-weave fabric or canvas. Position the tops of the trees in the center of the canvas as shown in the diagram. Stitch each tree from the top down as diagramed. Fill in between the branches of each tree as diagramed. For the background around the trees, the recommended stitch is basketweave. The finished pattern measures 11″ square on #14 canvas.

Magnolia

This flower pattern dates from the last quarter of the nineteenth century. Each flower's three segments were traditionally worked in white with green leaves against a blue background. Our addition of more colors brings gaiety and excitement to the design, although it lessens the resemblance to the magnolia itself.

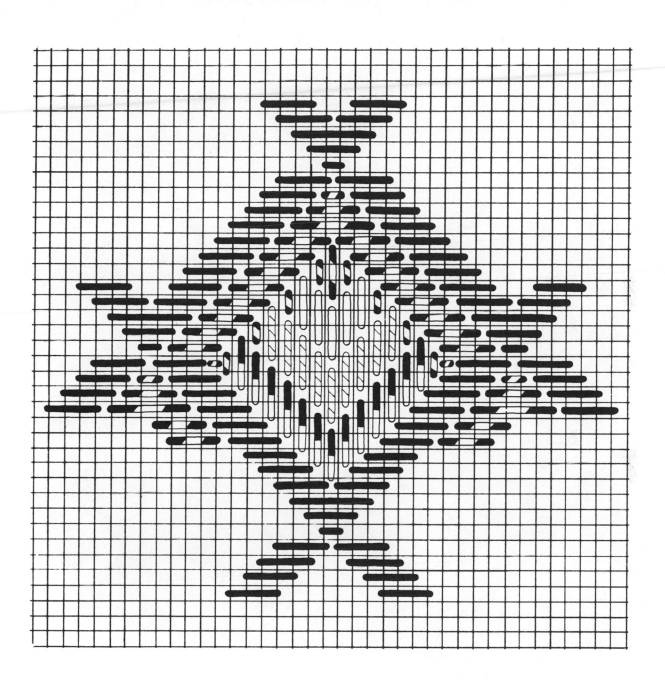

Stitching Directions. We have worked the solid black stitches in the diagram in green to represent the leaves. Each flower block is a diamond. The flower stitches are worked vertically. The leaves and background are stitched horizontally. Work all the leaves first; then fill in the flowers and background. The finished piece measures 7½″ square on #14 canvas.

Chrysanthemum

In early America, the average woman had few artistic outlets. She could garden, she could embroider, and she could quilt. It comes as no surprise then, that many quilt patterns are named after garden flowers, regardless of whether they resemble their namesakes.

The Chrysanthemum design dates from the beginning of the twentieth century. It closely resembles Swing in the Center and Eight Hands Round, pattern names derived from square dancing. Most "new" quilt designs in the late nineteenth century were, in fact, variations and elaborations on patterns already in existence. But because designing a "new" quilt pattern was a status symbol, women

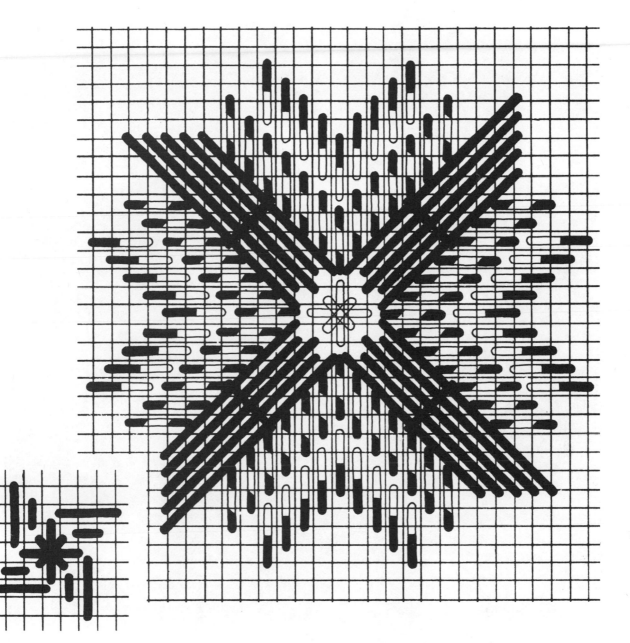

took the patterns they knew and tried to improve them.

Stitching Directions. Start in the center of a flower, and work a double straight cross stitch (#13). Then work straight stitches in concentric *V*s as diagramed. Each arm of the dark *X* is composed of 5 long stitches stretching from the flower's center to its tip. Tack down the long stitches with 2 smaller (couching) stitches as diagramed. Work all flowers. Adjoining flowers touch at the tips of their smallest *V*s. Place background pinwheels so that each pinwheel blade touches one arm of a dark *X*. Complete the background in basketweave. The finished piece measures 7″ square on #14 canvas.

Dutch Rose

The Dutch Rose was one of several patterns often used for Album quilts, which were made at Friendship quilting bees. Each guest would work one patch and sign it with india ink or in cross stitch on the plain background spaces. Then the patches were joined together and quilted to form a presentation quilt for a dear friend or departing minister.

The Dutch Rose is a close cousin of the Duck Paddle (page 174). If the four duck feet of that design are pushed together so that they touch, they form a Dutch Rose.

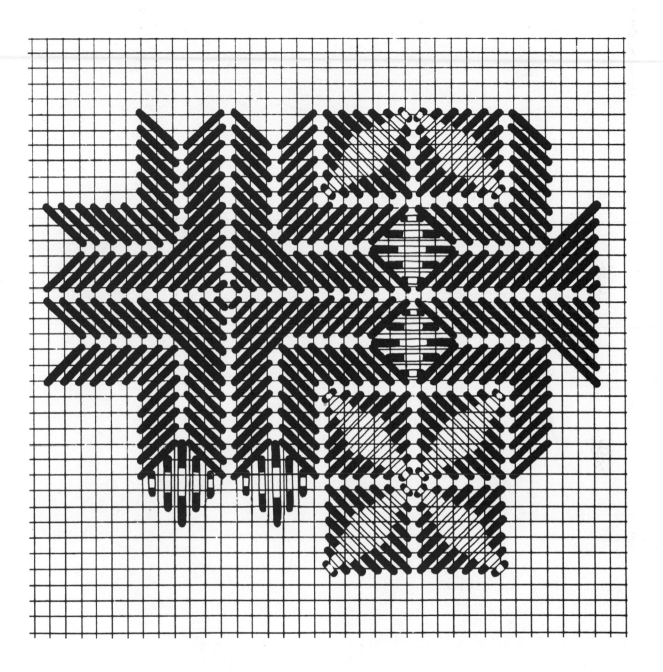

Stitching Directions. Each rose is composed of 8 layered *L*s that touch each other. Begin at the center of each rose, and stitch as diagramed. The finished piece measures 7½″ square on #14 canvas.

Flower Baskets

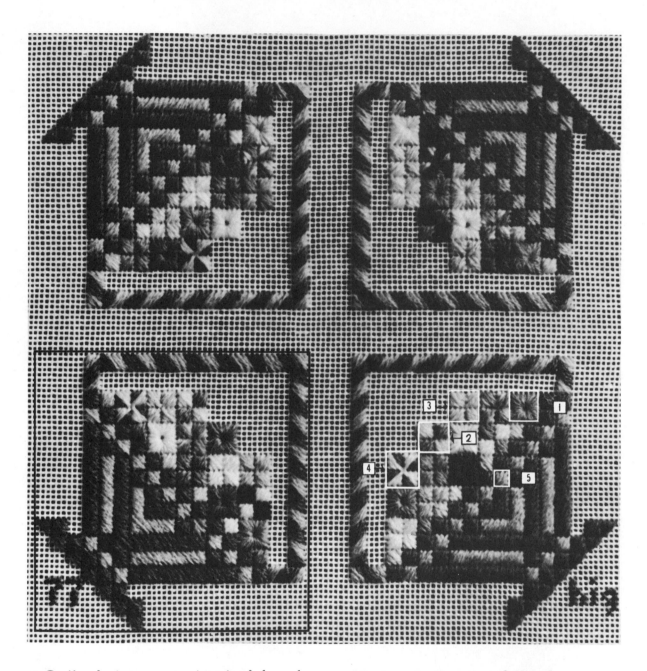

Quilt designs were inspired by objects found within the home as well as by nature without. An example of such a design is the Flower Baskets pattern.

Baskets were very popular quilt motifs, and usually named for what the basket contained; for example, Cherry Baskets or Cactus Baskets.

Notice that some of the flowers are based on the same pinwheel pattern used in Broken Dishes (page 78) and Whirligig (page 180). The baskets could face outward to form a complementary design, as in Spring Garden (page 46).

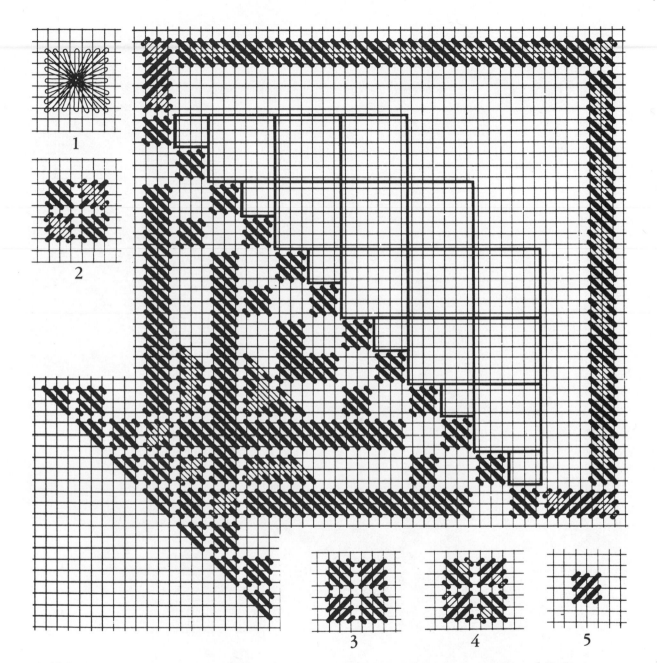

1

2

3   4   5

Stitching Directions. The basket handles pictured are 9 threads apart. Work the handles and baskets as diagramed. Because each basket is worked on the diagonal, be careful with stitch tension. This pattern is best worked on a frame to minimize canvas distortion.

Fill the baskets with multicolored flowers. Place large and small flowers as indicated on the diagram. The square (Algerian eye) flower is worked in the same manner as the diamond eye (#12), with all stitches meeting in the center hole. The recommended background stitch is basketweave. The finished piece measures 9″ square on #14 canvas.

American Flag

America's early days were precarious. The new land had barely won its independence and was struggling. The young nation survived because of the pride of its citizens in their Republic. This pride showed itself clearly in decorative arts. Eagles, stars, and flags appeared on woodwork, furniture, and quilts.

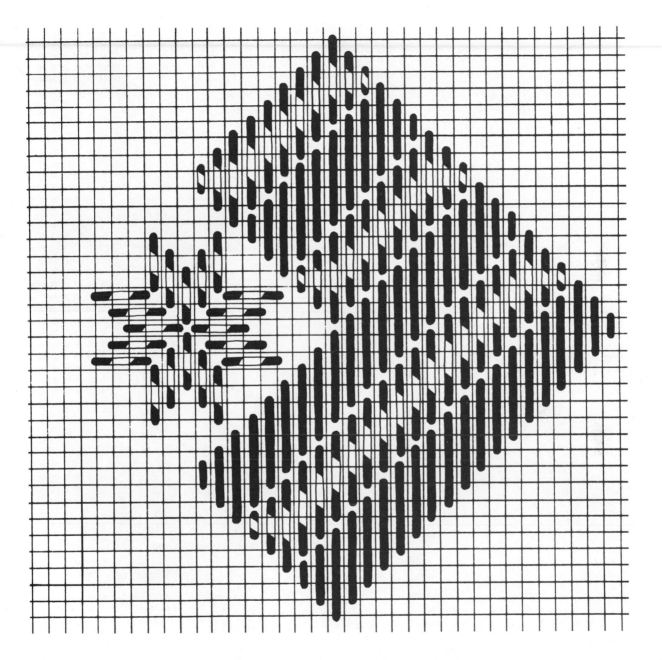

Stitching Directions. Begin each flag by stitching the top white stripe. Complete the stripes and star as diagramed. Work the blue field in basketweave. Complete background with basketweave or Hungarian. For another background possibility, see Ships at Sea (page 68), in which the background is stitched in the same manner as the design itself. The finished piece measures 11″ square on #14 canvas.

Confederate Star

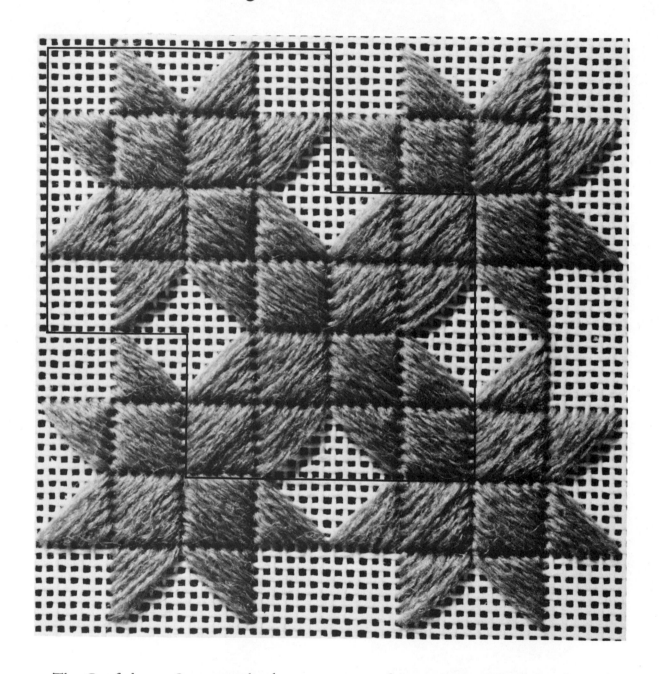

The Confederate Star was also known as Devil's Claws. Whether the Confederate Star pattern was devised during the Civil War or in memory of it, we do not know. The pattern is actually composed of five stars; the central star shares two of its points with each of the four corner stars.

During the Civil War emotion ran high in the South, and quilts were stitched honoring the Confederacy both in name and in pattern.

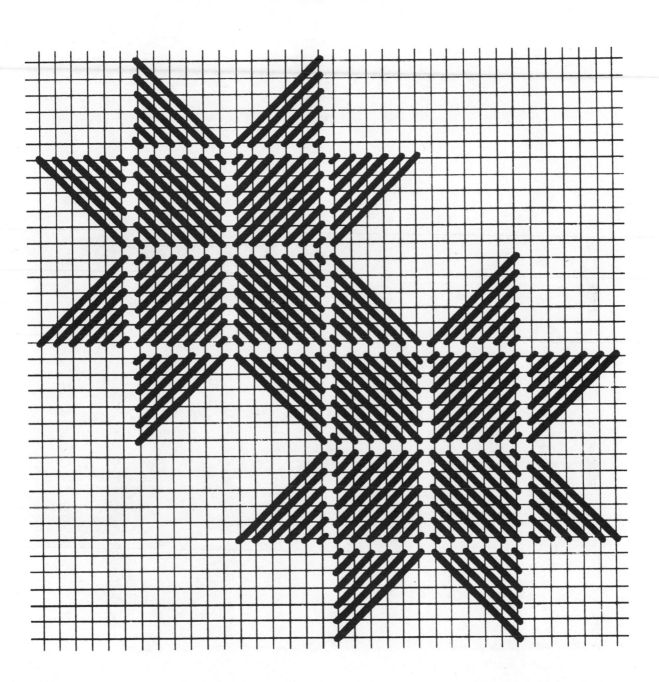

Stitching Directions. Begin in the center of the canvas. Work stars as diagramed. Work the background in basketweave, Hungarian, or flat stitches. The finished piece measures 4″ square on #14 canvas.

Caning

Weaving seems to have been a prehistoric skill that developed from basketry. Early humans wove rushes and canes into mats and baskets. As the fibers chosen grew thinner, this work became finer and more pliable until cloth developed. Some linens found in Egyptian tombs have many more threads per square inch than do our finest percales today.

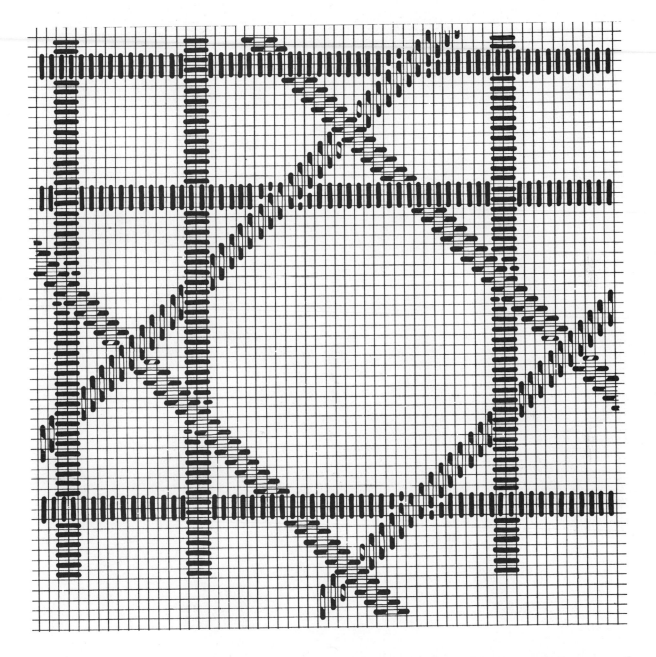

Stitching Directions. This pattern has been stitched on evenweave fabric. It should be worked on a frame. Begin at the top left corner. Keep outside edges smooth, as photographed. (The diagram shows continuations of the pattern on all sides.) Complete the pattern as diagramed, taking careful note of which cane is on top at each intersection. If you work this pattern in needlepoint, the recommended background is basketweave. The pattern measures 9½" square on evenweave fabric with 16 threads per inch.

Woven Rushes

Another primitive basketry technique that may have influenced the development of cloth was the weaving of rushes. There are over 250 varieties of these relatives of grasses, and they are found in marshy spots throughout the temperate zones. In medieval times, before the advent of carpeting, rushes and sweet herbs were strewn on floors to form a soft, insulating mat.

In America's early days, dried rushes were dipped in scalding grease to form a rude candle called a *rushlight*. They gave good, clear illumination. A rushlight two feet long would burn for nearly an hour.

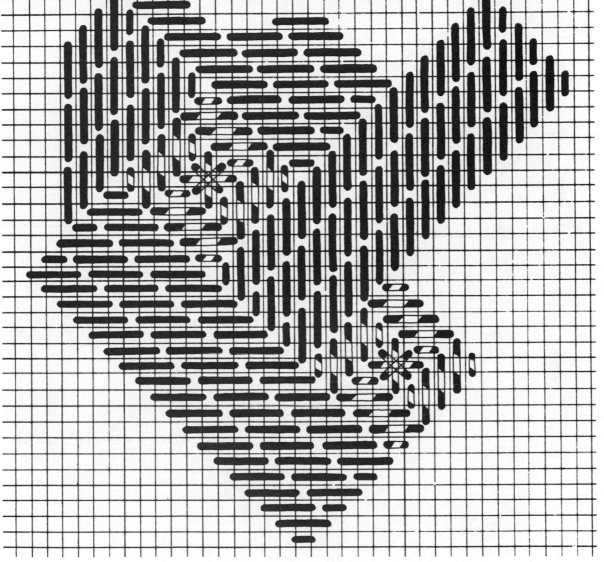

Stitching Directions. Begin at the center of a background diamond with double straight cross stitch (#13). Complete the background diamond as diagramed. Next work all the woven rushes. Then fill in the background with additional diamonds. The finished piece measures 7″ square on #14 canvas.

Ships at Sea

To those who lived along the shores of the Atlantic and the Great Lakes, sailing ships were a way of life. Survival often depended upon fishing or trading. Many women spent large parts of their lives looking toward the horizon and praying for their menfolk's safe return.

In this pattern, the negative (background) spaces have been stitched in the same manner as the design itself. The ships seem to be emerging from a fog bank into the bright sunshine.

Stitching Directions. Stitch the boat first. Work the sails as diagramed; the right sail mirrors the left, reversing the stitch direction. Stitch the water. Fill in the sky to complete the diamond. Stitch mast over center of sails with chain stitch or backstitch, using 1 strand of yarn. Complete by stitching the background as photographed. Do not use the sail color as the background color. Other possible background stitches are basketweave, Hungarian, or straight Milanese. The finished piece measures 11″ square on #14 canvas.

Baskets

Basket patterns were popular nineteenth-century quilt designs because they could be arranged in many ways on a quilt. In this composition, the background spaces form a design equal in strength to that of the baskets themselves.

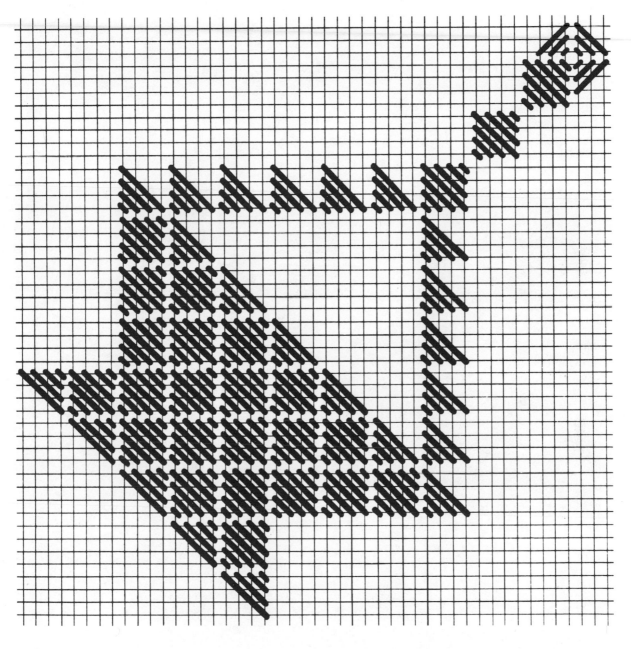

Stitching Directions. This pattern is stitched on evenweave fabric and should be worked on a frame. The tops of four basket handles meet to form a central square. Stitch each basket from the top down as diagramed. Note that basket bottoms surround a background diamond. In needlepoint, the recommended background stitch is basketweave. The finished piece measures 11″ square on evenweave fabric with 16 threads per inch.

Sailboats

Sailboats is another quilt design in which individual pictorial modules join together to form a whole much more fascinating than the module itself. The individual sailboats, though recognizable, are nothing special. But when joined together, they produce an overall design of great fascination and appeal. The general effect is strong, with a kaleidoscopic or American Indian feel to it.

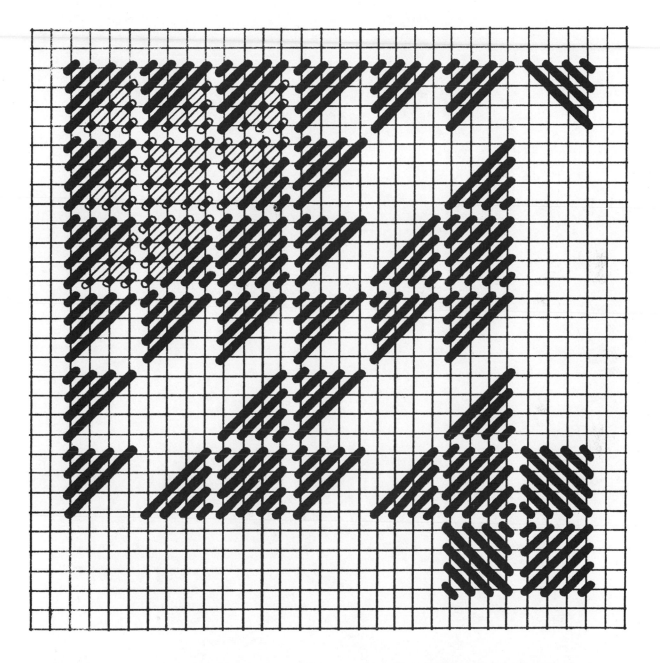

Stitching Directions. Start at upper left corner of graph (which corresponds to the upper left corner of the photograph), and stitch as diagramed. The dark stitches on the graph correspond to the light stitches in the photograph. Be careful to work with an even tension be- cause all stitches in each quadrant are worked on the same diagonal direction. This pattern should be worked on a frame to minimize distortion of the canvas. The finished piece measures 11″ square on #14 canvas.

Blazing Star

Some pictorial patterns give the effect of the object represented rather than an exact picture of it. Blazing Star, also known as Sunburst, is such an impressionistic design.

The isolated inhabitants of the American frontier depended on the world around them for any artistic inspirations. Neighbors were far away, and mass communications had not yet made it possible for women in one portion of the country to know what women in another section were producing. The sun and the stars in the sky overhead inspired the design and the name of this quilt pattern.

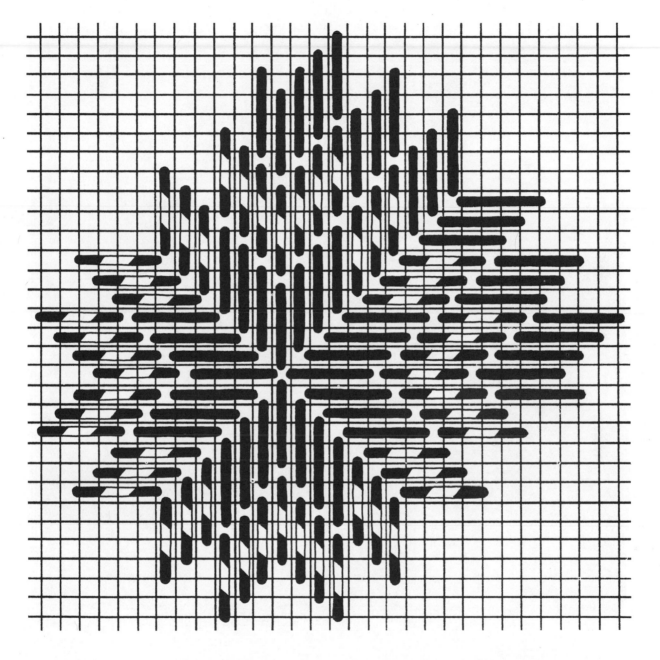

Stitching Directions. Begin by stitching the central star as diagramed. Work concentric rings around star, finishing each ring before beginning the next. Continue adding rings until the star is as large as you wish. The finished piece measures 10″ square when worked on #14 canvas.

Courthouse Steps

After the Civil War, newspapers and magazines reached the farthest corners of the nation. The era of mass communications had begun. Quilt patterns appeared in such publications as *Godey's Lady's Book,* and from coast to coast, American women pieced them.

The favorite quilt designs in this era were the crazy quilt and the Log Cabin, in all its forms. Courthouse Steps was one such variation. Because it can be worked in many colors, Courthouse Steps is a wonderful way to utilize leftover yarn.

Stitching Directions. Start in the center of the canvas, and stitch as diagramed. The more colors you use, the easier it is to avoid having two adjoining diamonds of the same color. Note that the diamonds touch in vertical rows and are separated in horizontal rows. The finished piece measures 11″ square on #14 canvas.

Broken Dishes

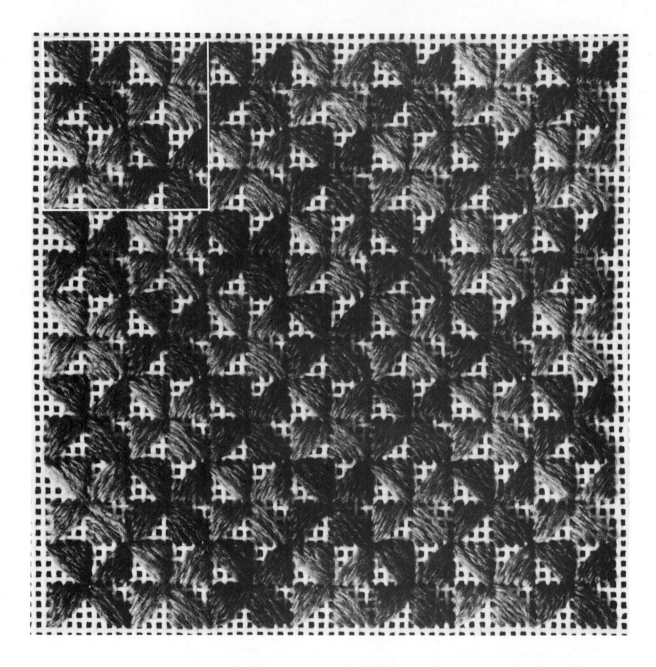

The Pinwheel or Flutter Wheel was one of the oldest of America's pieced quilt patterns. When many pinwheels touched each other, the pattern was called Broken Dishes. The sharp corners of broken crockery were obviously just as memorable in our ancestors' time as they are in ours.

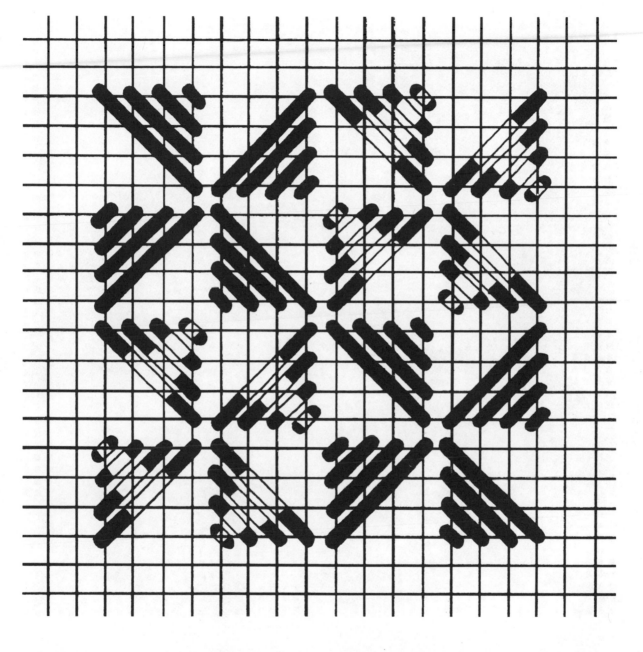

Stitching Directions. Start working Broken Dishes with darker color in the upper left corner of canvas, and stitch as diagramed. Fill in lighter-color pinwheels and then fill in background by completing each flat stitch. The photographed piece measures 4″ square on #14 canvas. The size of each pinwheel can be enlarged if a bolder pattern is desired.

Twin Sisters

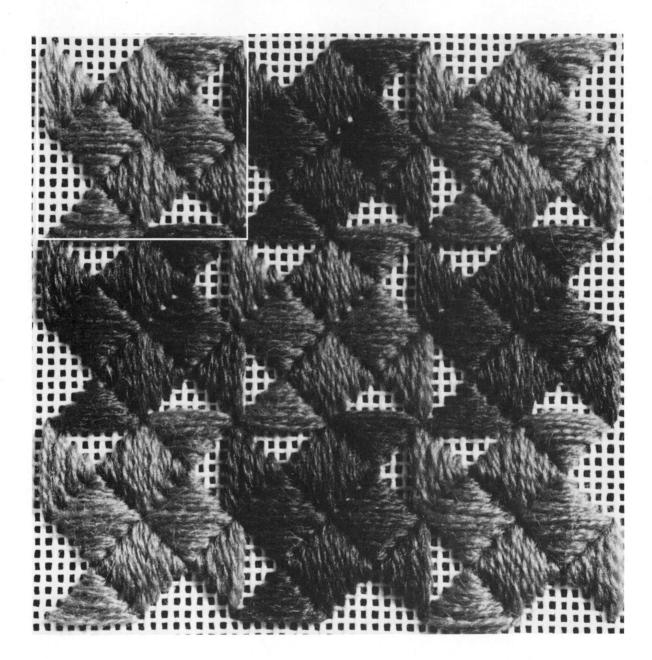

The Pinwheel variations that form this pattern create an interconnecting design that has great movement. This eighteenth-century pattern is based on a design called Windmill, which was also known as Water Mill and Mill Wheel.

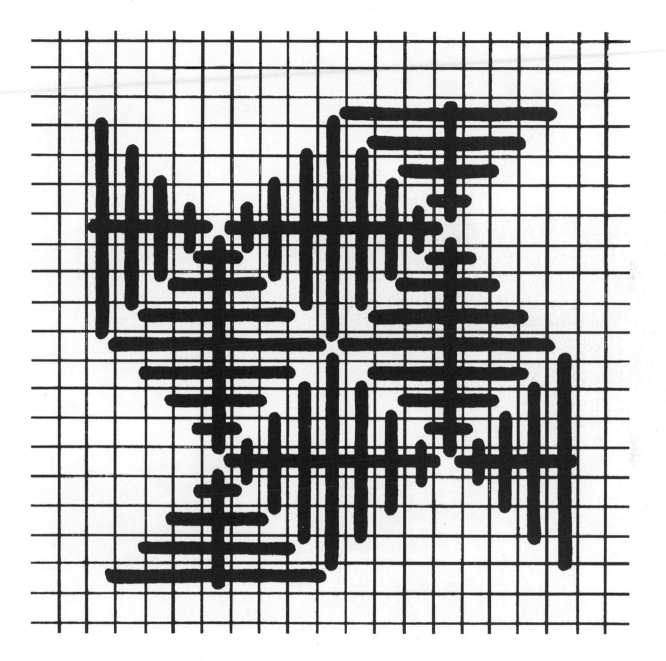

Stitching Directions. Start with lighter color in upper left corner of canvas. In each segment, work 1 long hidden stitch first. Cover it with perpendicular stitches as diagramed. Note that adjoining pinwheels share all corner holes. Fill in the background by completing empty triangles within the design with three straight stitches. The photographed piece measures 4″ square on #14 canvas.

Broad Arrow

American pioneers had to face such hard realities as sickness, hunger, and Indians. When the farmers plowed each spring, they turned up arrowheads, which had been heaved out of the ground by winter frosts.

The pattern formed by these interlocking arrowheads is reminiscent of the work of such modern artists as M. C. Escher.

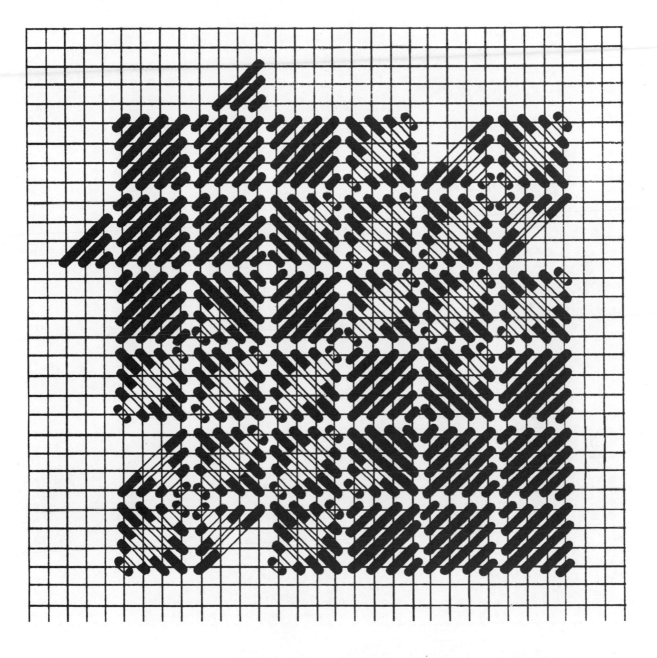

Stitching Directions. Work all light-colored arrows first, as diagramed. Note that these arrows touch tip to tip and bottom to bottom on one diagonal and that they touch side to side on the other diagonal and point in alternate directions. Fill in with dark arrows to complete the pattern. The finished piece measures 4″ on #14 canvas.

Box Quilt

This Box Quilt design is one example of the many three-dimensional box designs that were popular in the nineteenth century. Easy stitching and a simple design with great depth accounted for the pattern's popularity.

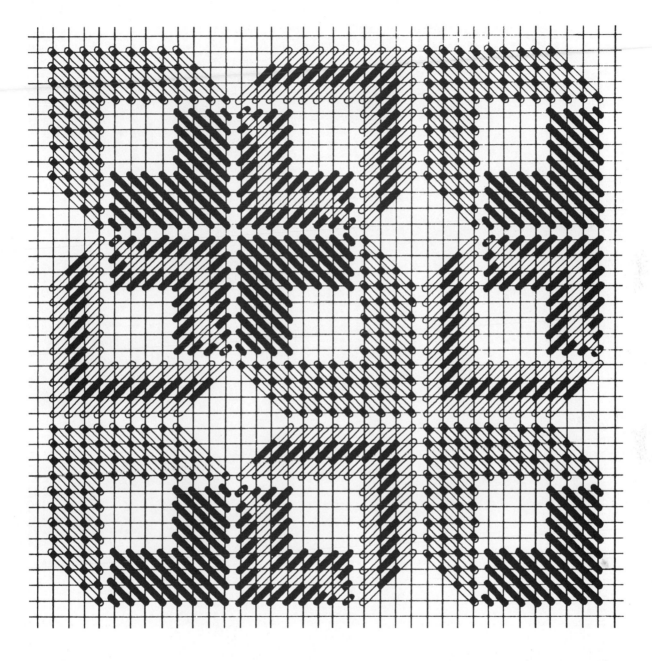

Stitching Directions. Begin in the upper left corner of canvas as photographed or where the corners of each 4-box unit meet in the center of the canvas. Stitch boxes as diagramed. The suggested background stitch is basketweave. The finished piece measures 4″ on #14 canvas.

Noon and Night

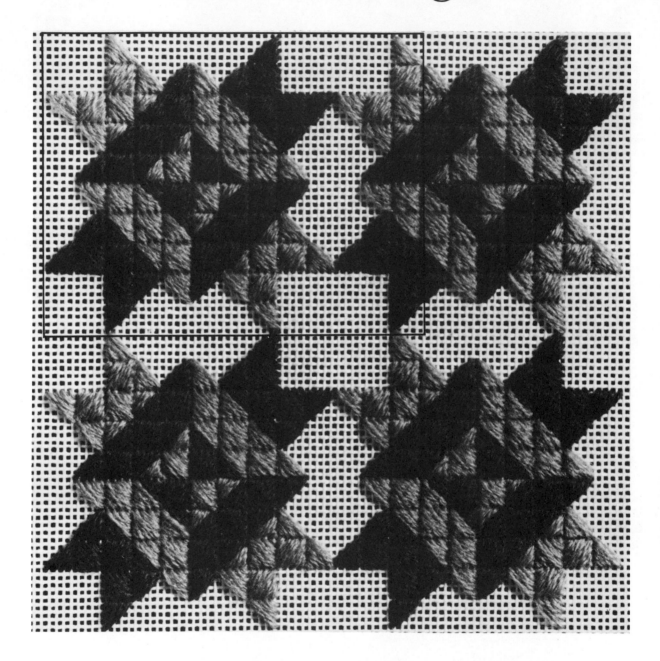

Noon and Night is a close relative of David and Goliath and Flying Darts. Rays of sunlight were often called *darts* in the romantic literature of the 1800s. The variation of tones from the light of noon to the dark of night may have inspired this pattern's name.

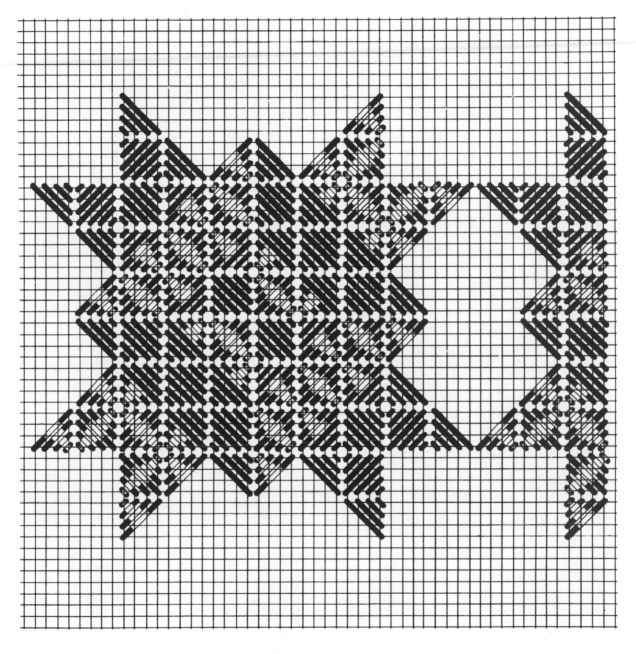

Stitching Directions. Start in the upper left corner of the canvas, or place the center of one design in the center of the canvas, and stitch as diagramed. To increase the size of the finished piece, add more designs. This pattern produces interesting negative space and would also work well on evenweave fabric. In needlepoint, the recommended background stitch is basketweave. The finished piece measures 6″ square on #14 canvas.

Road to Tennessee

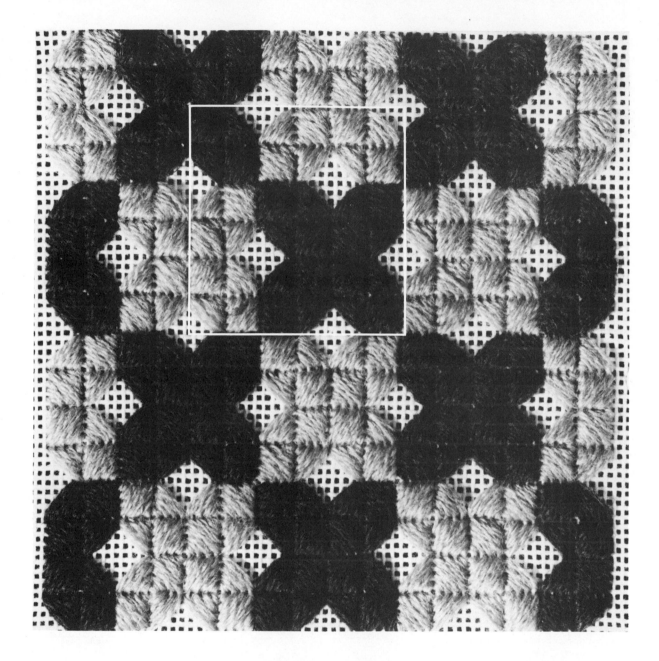

Colonial Americans lived along a narrow strip of land between the Atlantic and the Appalachians. The English would not allow them to move across mountains and risk war by invading French territory. But after the Revolution, the lure of new land drew settlers farther and farther west.

Tennessee became a state in 1796, after the Cherokee Indians had been subdued. Settlers moved west into the state from North Carolina and Virginia, and the road to Tennessee played a vital role in their lives.

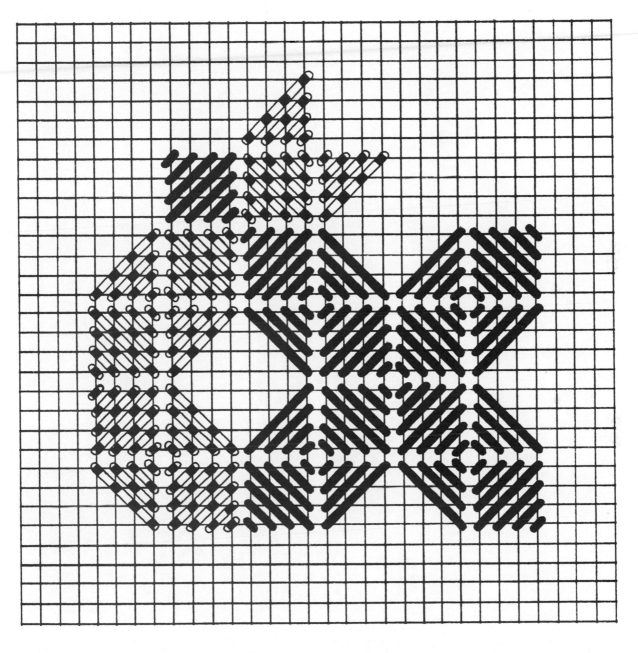

Stitching Directions. Begin in the center of the canvas and work one *X* as diagramed. Complete all *X*s of the same color. Fill with *X*s of the second color. The suggested background stitch is basketweave. The finished piece measures 5″ square on #14 canvas.

Road to California

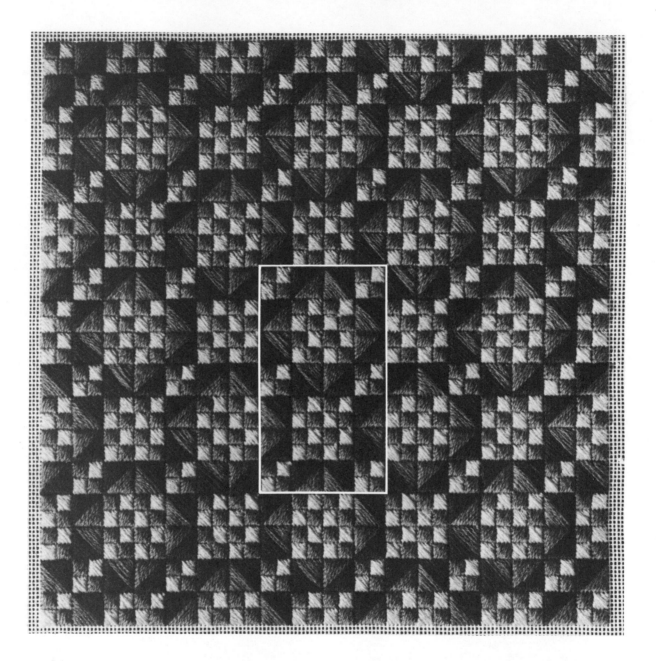

Another road, a much longer one, was the road to California. After the close of the Mexican War in 1845, Mexico ceded California to the United States. It became a state five years later. In the twelve months following the discovery of gold at Sutter's Mill in 1848, 42,000 Americans crossed 2,000 miles of plains and mountains in Conestoga wagons. The deep ruts made by wagon wheels can sometimes still be seen in the Western states. California's population grew from 5,000 in 1845 to 380,000 twelve years later. The road to California was a very real one to our ancestors, and many of them died along it.

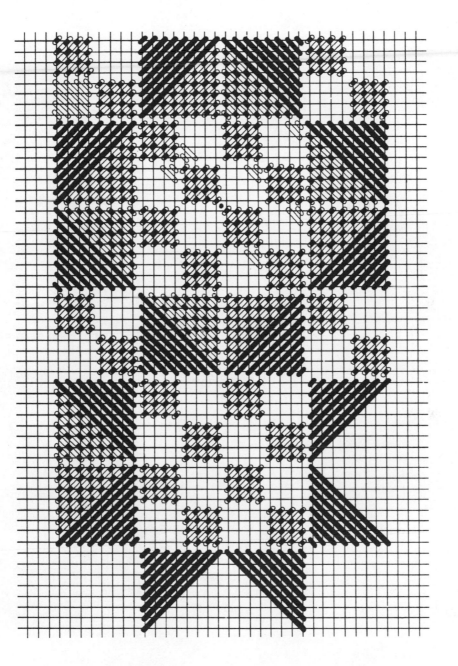

Stitching Directions. Begin in center of canvas at center mark, and stitch as diagramed. The finished piece measures 11″ square on #14 canvas.

Winged Square

The Winged Square is also called the Golden Gate. It was popular among pioneer women as a bridal quilt pattern about the time of the California gold rush. Winged Square quilts were un-doubtedly carried west in Conestoga wagons, which may account for the pattern's second name. It is an open, delicate design that lends itself well to stitching on evenweave fabric.

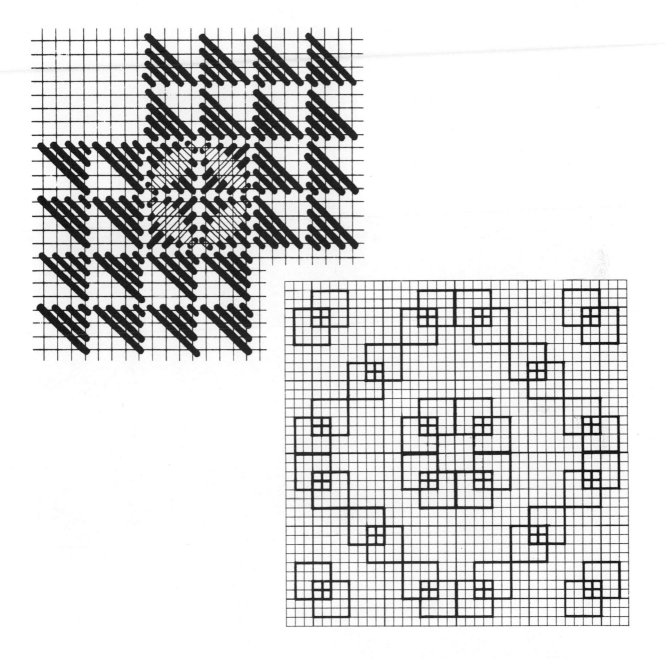

Stitching Directions. This pattern is stitched on evenweave fabric and should be worked on a frame. Begin at the center of the cloth, and work 4 modules as diagramed and outlined. If you are working in needlepoint, fill in the empty spaces within each winged square with the background color. The remaining background can be worked in two-direction flat stitch or the basket-weave. The finished piece measures 9″ square on evenweave fabric with 16 threads per inch.

Star and Chain

The Star and Chain is also known as Ring around the Star, Brunswick Star, and Rolling Star. It dates from the middle of the nineteenth century and creates a wonderful optical illusion. The more you look at it, the more new patterns you see. This design would make a per-fect octagonal pillow; just leave off the corners.

Stitching Directions. Begin in the center, and stitch star as diagramed. Work the smaller chain as diagramed, noting that it touches each tip of the

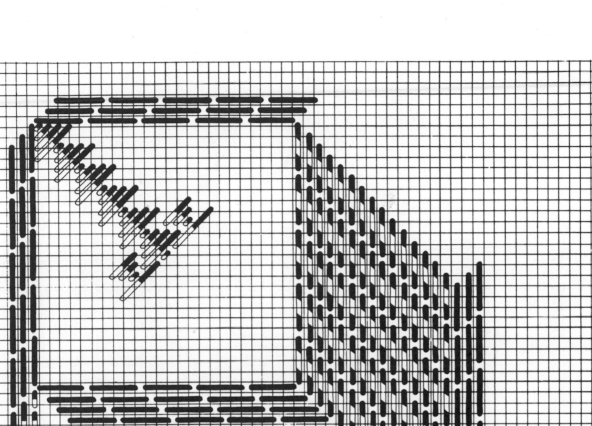

star. Each smaller chain diamond is formed of 5 ribs of 16 stitches each. Work the larger chain as pictured; note that it touches the smaller chain. Each section of the larger chain is formed of 6 ribs of 26 stitches each. All stitches in all chains are identical.

Work the octagonal background around star in basketweave. Fill the remaining background triangles with straight Milanese and diagonal Milanese as diagramed. Begin working each background triangle at the peak (right

See overall diagram on page 96.

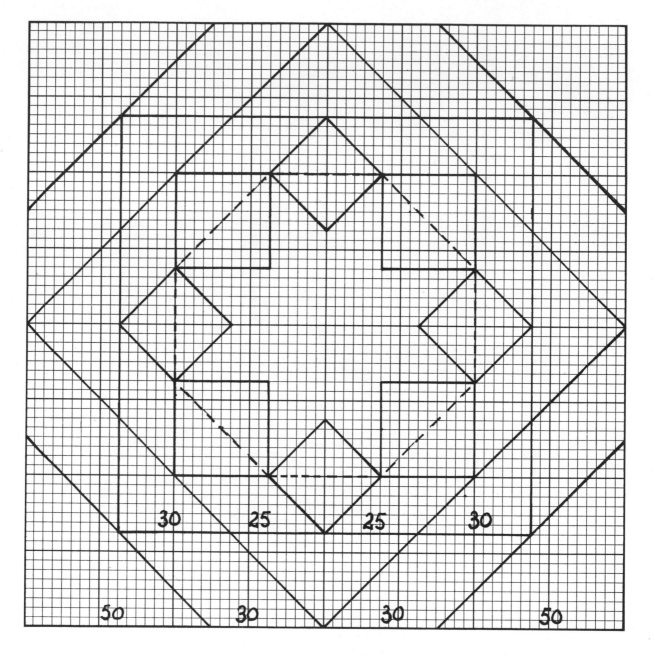

angle); refer to the photograph for the proper direction of the stitches in each triangle. The numbers on the overall diagram indicate the number of threads in each area. This design would also work well on evenweave fabric. The finished piece is 12″ square on #14 canvas.

Amish Quilts

Quilts stitched by women of the Amish religious sect during the past 100 years have great appeal to us today. Their unusual use of color and simple geometric shapes are reminiscent of contemporary paintings and graphics, and the needlework in them is of superb quality.

The Amish sect originated in Switzerland after the Protestant Reformation. Its members were persecuted in Europe, and in 1727, William Penn offered them land in Pennsylvania. Amish immigration continued until 1850. Although early settlements were located in Pennsylvania, later ones branched out into the developing Middle West.

Historically, the Amish have chosen a "plain and simple" style of life. They are peaceful and self-sufficient. They live in the world around them and yet are not of it. Non-Amish, whatever their nationality, are called the *English*.

Amish communities wish to lead peaceful lives according to their beliefs and without interference from the outside world. They do not use electricity, modern clothing, the automobile, television, or indoor plumbing. Their rejection of buttons, which to them symbolized the military, led to their being nicknamed *hookers*. It is within this tradition of peaceful isolation that Amish quilting developed.

Few, if any, Amish quilts were pieced before 1860. Perhaps their lives were not settled enough before that time, or perhaps Amish bishops prohibited quilt making as an "English" custom. This was the height of America's quilting era, and Amish women must have been aware of the beauty being created by non-Amish women around them. After 1860, they took what they had seen and translated it into their own terms.

Amish quilts, like all American pieced quilts, were composed of sewing scraps and usable patches cut from worn-out clothes. The Amish called them "quilts to use up." Although the Amish historically prohibited printed textiles, they allowed the use of colored cloth. Therefore, no printed fabrics were used in Amish quilts.

By 1860, when the Amish first began quilting, the sewing machine had been invented, and it soon became part of their quilting tradition. Almost all Amish quilts were machine-pieced and then hand-quilted with tiny stitches that could number twenty stitches to the inch.

Perhaps because they understood the limitations of the treadle sewing machine, Amish women formed their quilts of large geometric shapes. Whatever the reason for their compositions, Amish quilt patterns are unique. Striped quilts such as Bars and central diamond patterns such as Diamond in Square are thoroughly Amish. Their piecing is simple, and their quilting, magnificent.

Amish women sometimes borrowed patterns from their "English" neighbors and translated these in their own way. Such translations include Barn Raising, Nine Patch, Diagonal Triangles, and Roman Stripe. What the outside world called Around the World, the Amish

changed and called Sunshine and
Shadow. This pattern is an excellent
Amish example of "quilts to use up."

The contrast between the plain and
simple composition of Amish quilts and
their rich, glowing colors and magnificent stitching appeals to us today.
These designs, cradled in simplicity,
exhibit sensitivity and sophistication.

STITCHING INFORMATION

In addition to the stitching diagrams,
we have provided overall diagrams for
several of the designs in this section.
The numbers on these diagrams indicate
the number of threads to be contained
within each area.

Diamond in Square

This characteristic Amish pattern is also known simply as Diamond or Center Diamond. It is an example of a quilt that begins in the middle and grows larger as additional pieces of cloth are added to it. The unwieldiness of this type of quilt as it neared completion must have made working on it very difficult.

Very fine quilting decorated these large, simple areas of color. The backs of fine Amish quilts, where only the quilting can be seen, are as beautiful as the fronts.

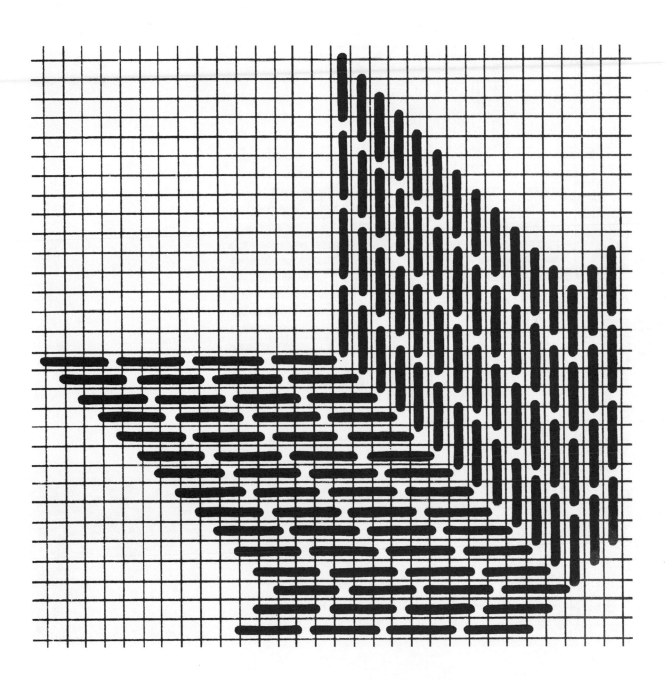

Stitching Directions on page 102.

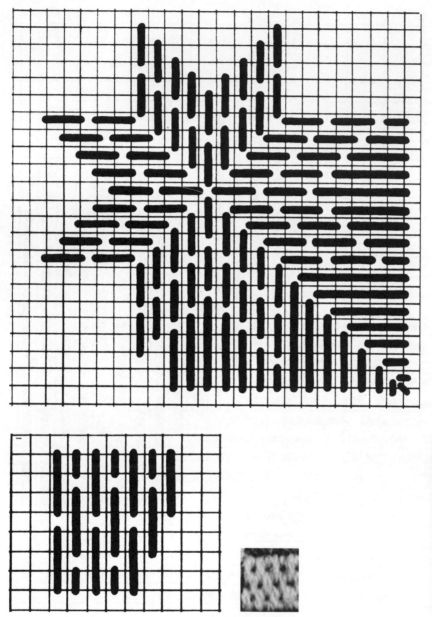

Stitching Directions. Stitch the central star in the center of the canvas as diagramed. Use basketweave to complete the diamond. Square off diamond with diagonal Milanese(#22) worked in from the peaks of the triangles to the center of each side of the diamond. Work small corner blocks in two-direction flat stitch (#15) at the tips of the central square. Connect small corner

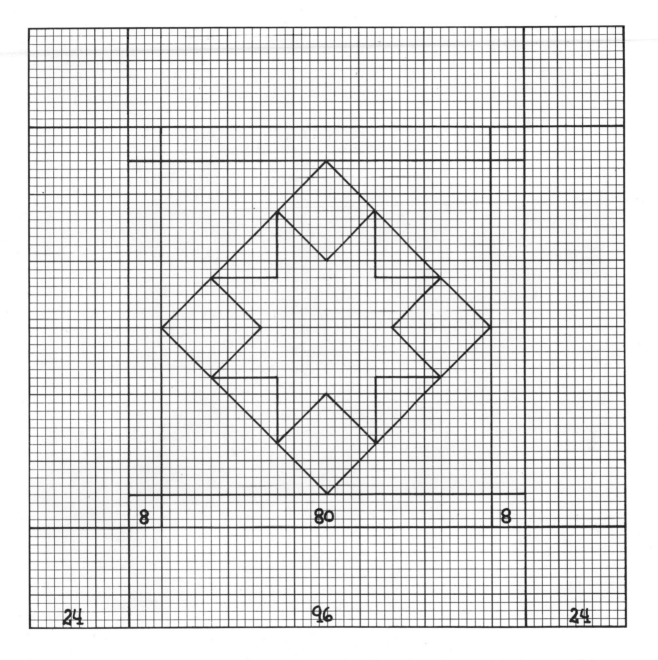

blocks with the brick stitch border as diagramed. Place the large corner blocks at tips of small corner blocks, and stitch as diagramed. Connect the large corner blocks with five-step bargello (#3).

Outline the piece with 1 row of long-armed cross (#19). The finished piece measures 11″ square on #14 canvas.

Bars

Amish names for quilt patterns were often as plain and simple as the quilts themselves. Striped quilts were sometimes pieced by non-Amish quilters in New England, but the form was not widely used. In the north of England, the striped pieced quilt is a well-known form, and such quilts are called *strippies*.

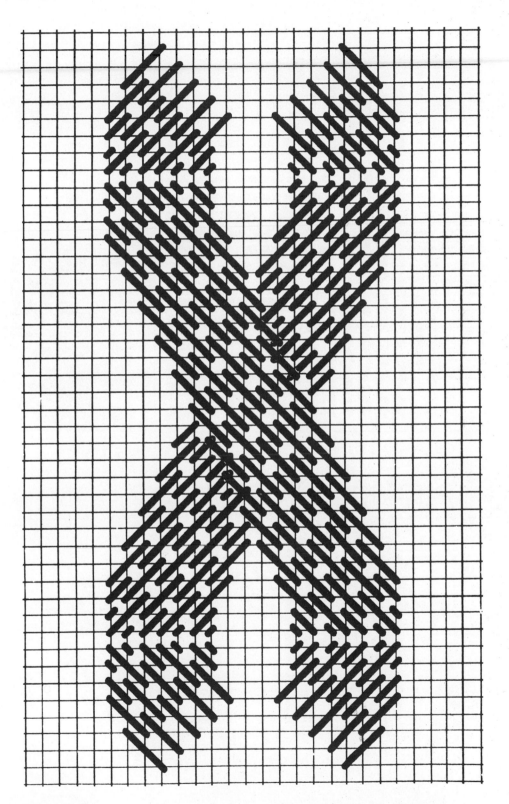

Stitching Directions on page 106.

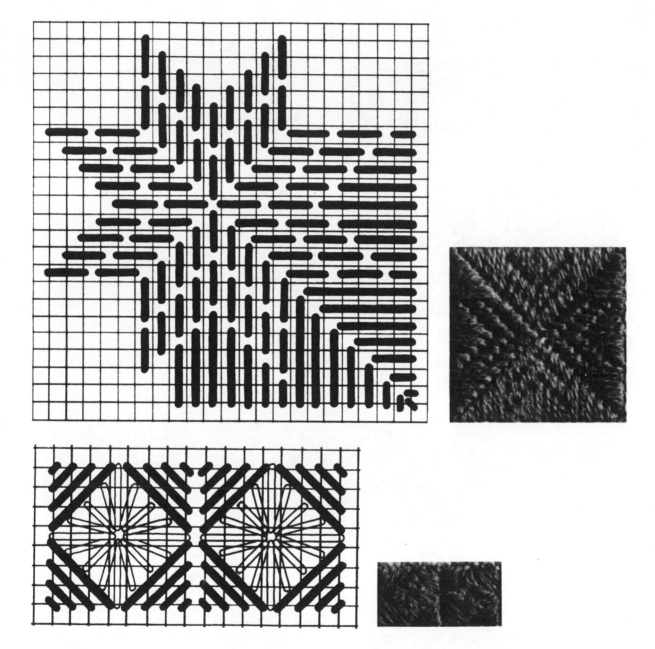

Stitching Directions. Determine the center of the canvas. Work diamond border around central square as diagramed. Each border side contains 11 diamonds. Work small blocks in two-direction flat stitch (#15) at each corner of this border. Work three cables inside central square. Two cables should touch the diamond border on the sides, and the third cable should be centered. Fill

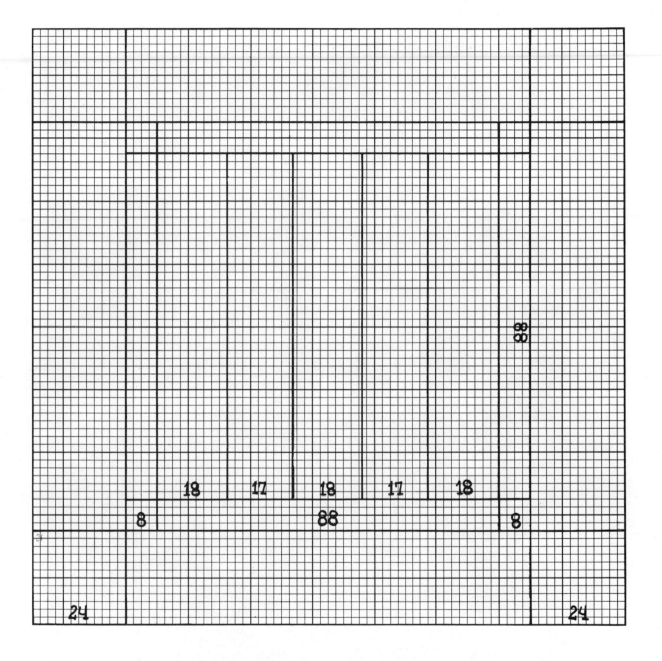

the two remaining bars with Hungarian (#18). Place the large corner blocks at tips of small corner blocks, and stitch as diagramed. Connect the large corner blocks with five-step bargello (#3). Outline piece with 1 row of long-armed cross (#19). The finished piece measures 12″ square on #14 canvas.

Nine-Patch

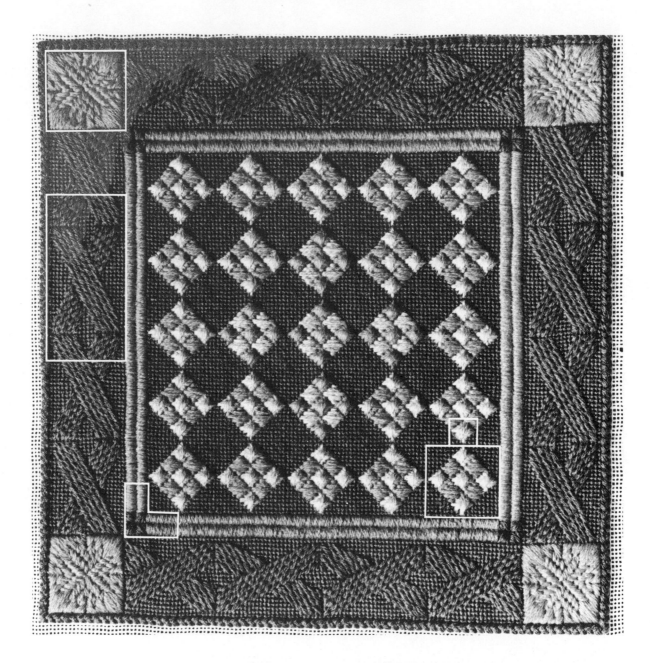

When Amish quilters borrowed from their *worldly* neighbors, the quilts that resulted bore a recognizably Amish stamp. Such a transformation took place with this pattern. The Nine-Patch was one of the basic designs in any American quilter's repertoire. When the pattern became Amish, the Nine-Patch blocks were placed within concentric borders. The same overall composition was used for Diamond in Square and Bars, but here the Nine-Patch blocks took the place of the more traditional Amish central designs.

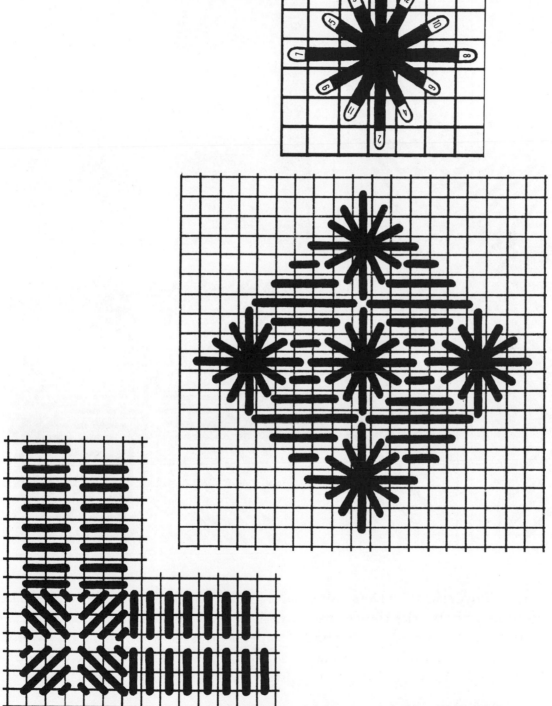

Stitching Directions on page 110.

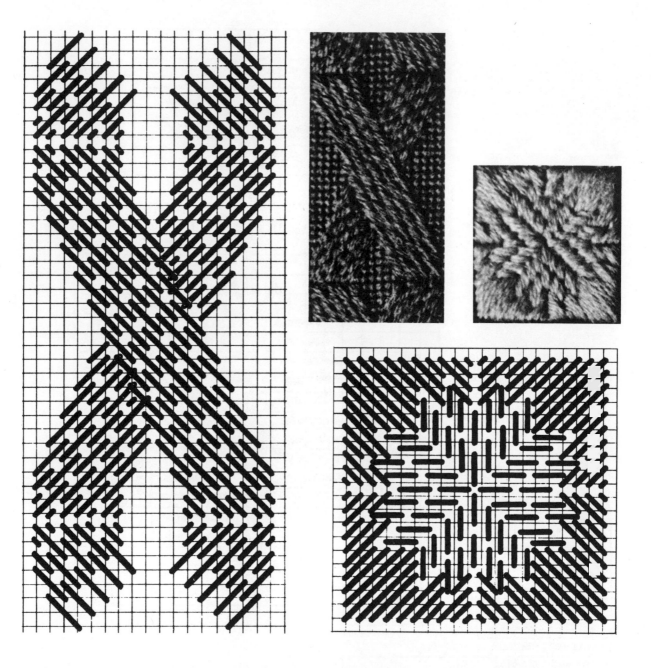

Stitching Directions. Determine center of canvas. Work the center Nine-Patch and the 4 Nine-Patches that touch its corners as diagramed. Reverse the colors and stitch the remaining 20 Nine-Patches. Fill in the central square with basketweave (#4). Work the small corner blocks at the tips of the central square, and connect them with an upright Gobelin border, as diagramed.

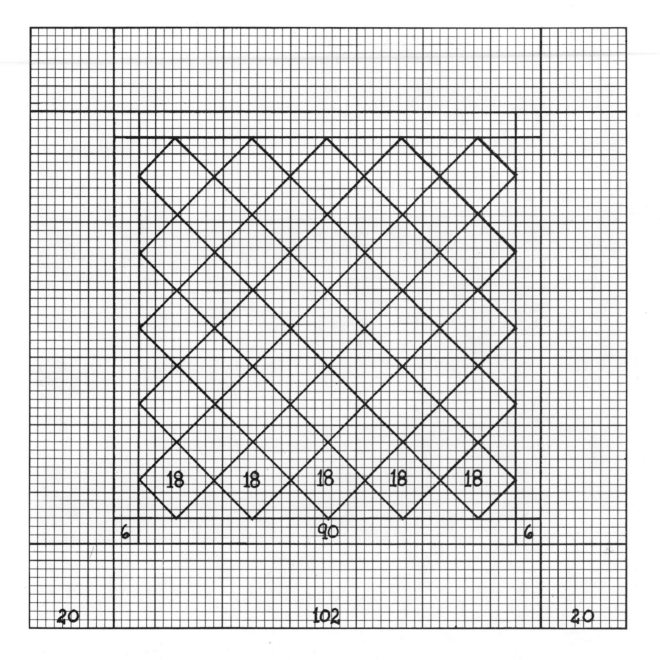

Place the large corner blocks at tips of small corner blocks, and stitch as diagramed. Connect the large corner blocks with a cable border, beginning each cable in the center of the border as photographed. Outline the piece with 1 row of long-armed cross (#19). The finished piece measures 11″ square on #14 canvas.

Sunshine and Shadow

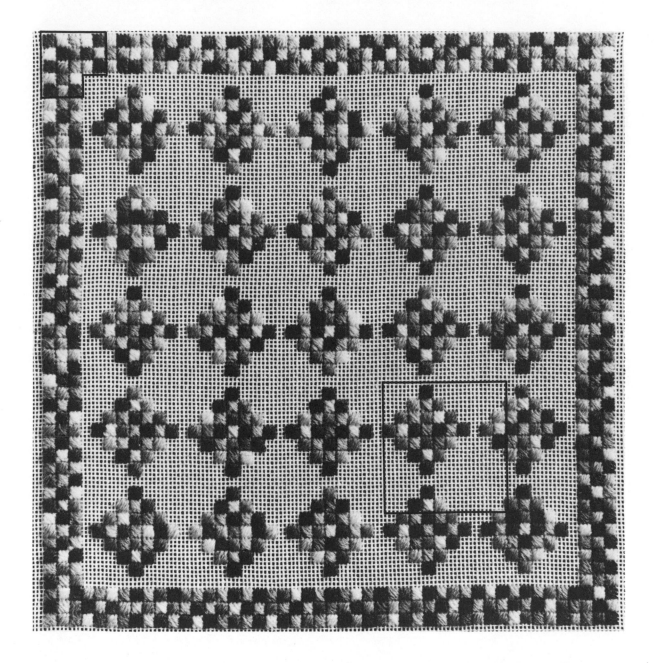

Sunshine and Shadow is another example of a worldly quilt pattern translated into Amish terms. The "English" called the design Around the World or Grandma's Dream. To the Amish, this was a wonderful "quilt to use up." It serves the same function in needlework as it does in quilting—creating beauty from otherwise useless bits and pieces.

Sunshine and Shadow alternates dark tones with light and bright hues. The result is a scintillating play of color.

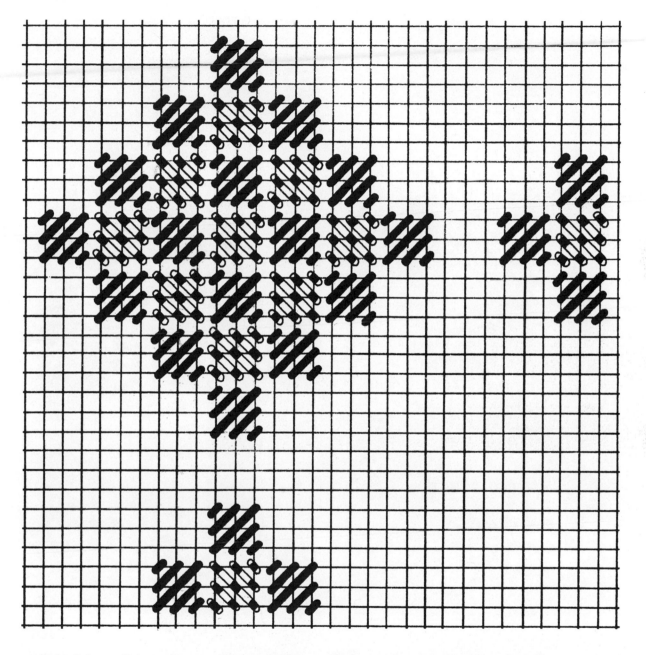

Stitching Directions. This design can be worked in two colors (as diagramed) or in many colors (as photographed). The more colors used, the easier their placement becomes. Begin in the center of the canvas, and stitch as diagramed. Stitch the border as diagramed (page 189). Suggested background stitches are the basketweave (#4) or the two-direction flat stitch (#15). The finished piece measures 11″ square on #14 canvas.

Diagonal Triangles

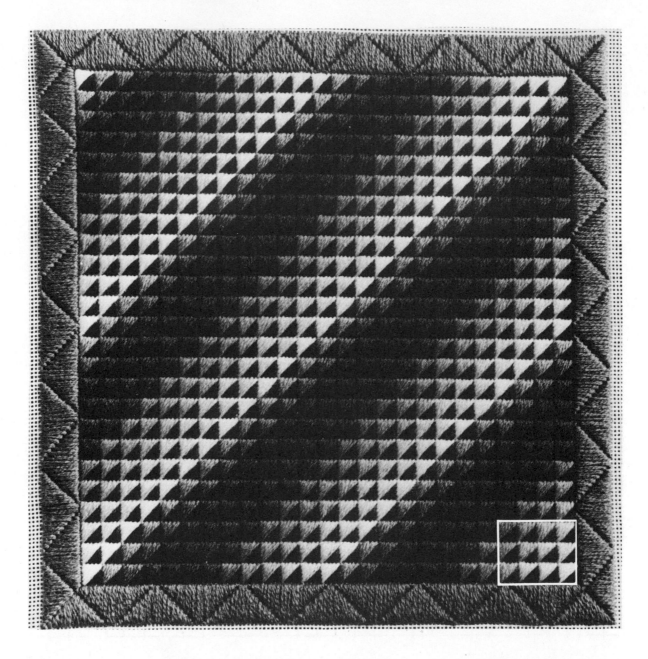

Diagonal Triangles is similar in its basic design to the Log Cabin patterns that were very popular with the "English." Each Log Cabin block was square and divided in half diagonally into dark and light triangles. These larger blocks closely resemble the much smaller blocks that are the basic components of Diagonal Triangles. The color choices and the traditional border give this pattern a distinctly Amish personality.

Stitching Directions. This spectrum is composed of thirteen colors. Begin by stitching a black triangle in the lower right corner as diagramed. Work 1 yellow triangle. Stitch 2 black triangles

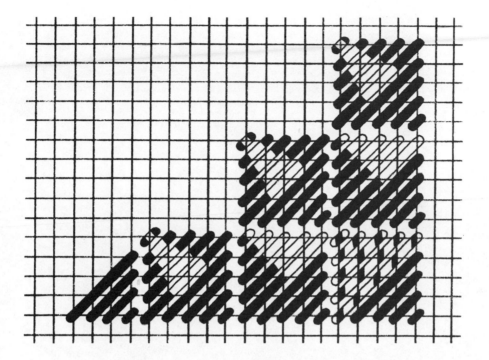

and then 2 yellow-orange triangles. Continue stitching black triangles alternating with colored triangles until the spectrum is completed with yellow green. Begin the second sequence with yellow triangles as photographed. This pattern should be worked on a frame because all the stitches pull the canvas in the same direction. The border is similar to the Spring Garden border (page 189). It is worked over 10 threads, with 2 stitches forming each triangle peak. Begin stitching the border at the center of each side. The finished piece measures 11" square on #14 canvas.

COMPARABLE YARN COLORS

APPLETON CREWEL	PATERNAYAN PERSIAN
998	050
551	458
555	Y40
557	965
444	958
446	240
502	231
504	221
105	612
747	330
645	367
545	520
253	545

Roman Stripe

A very early worldly quilt pattern was called Roman Stripe or Fence Posts. Cloth strips of different colors were sewed together to form broad bands of horizontal stripes. When the Amish formed triangles of such stripes, the result was the Roman Stripe pattern. The dark triangles remain undivided and serve as a somber background against which the bright stripes sparkle. The composition is very similar to that of Diagonal Triangles.

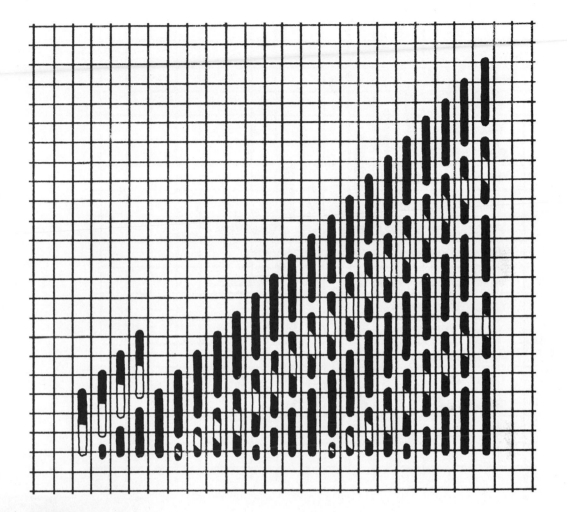

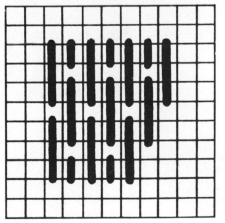

Stitching Directions on page 118.

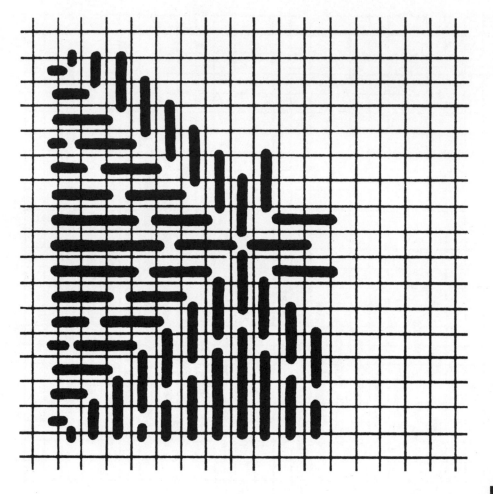

Stitching Directions. Stitch Roman Stripe blocks as diagramed. Both dark and colored stripes are stitched in the same way. Work the small corner blocks at tips of central square in the two-direction flat stitch. (#15). Connect small corner blocks with brick border as diagramed. Work the large corner

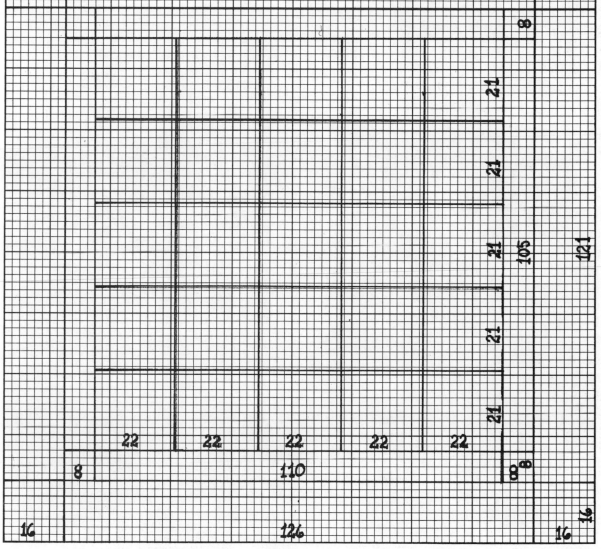

blocks as diagramed. Connect with five-step bargello (#3). Outline the piece with 1 row of long-armed cross (#19). The finished piece measures 12″ square on #14 canvas.

Hole in the Barn Door

Hole in the Barn Door had many names when it was pieced by worldly stitchers. Double Monkey Wrench, Love Knot, Puss in the Corner, Shoo Fly, Lincoln's Platform, and Sherman's March are a few of its aliases. But intriguing as these names are, the only one that describes what the design looks like is the plain and simple Amish choice, Hole in the Barn Door.

Amish patterns lend themselves to bright, modern colors. This pattern was stitched in such colors rather than in the more traditional, somber Amish tones.

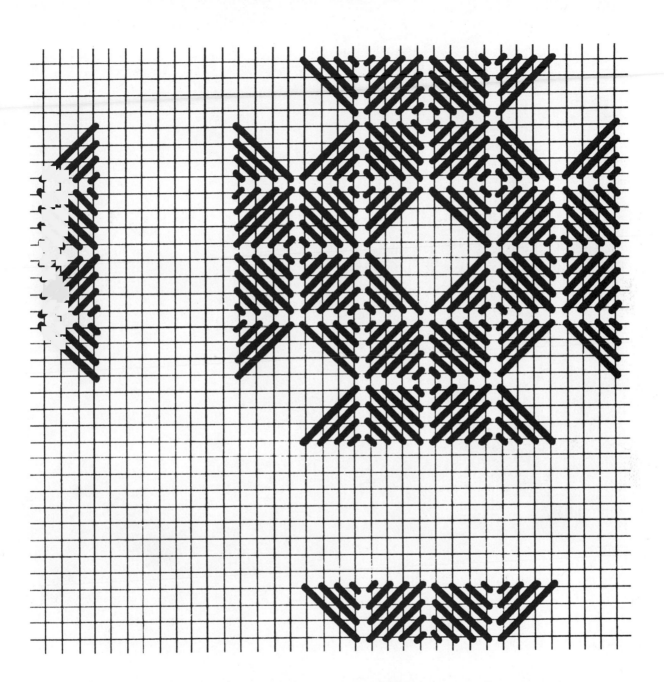

Stitching Directions. Stitch pattern as diagramed. Suggested background stitches are basketweave (#4), Hungarian (#18), or two-direction flat stitch (#15). The finished piece measures 10″ square on #14 canvas.

Bow Ties

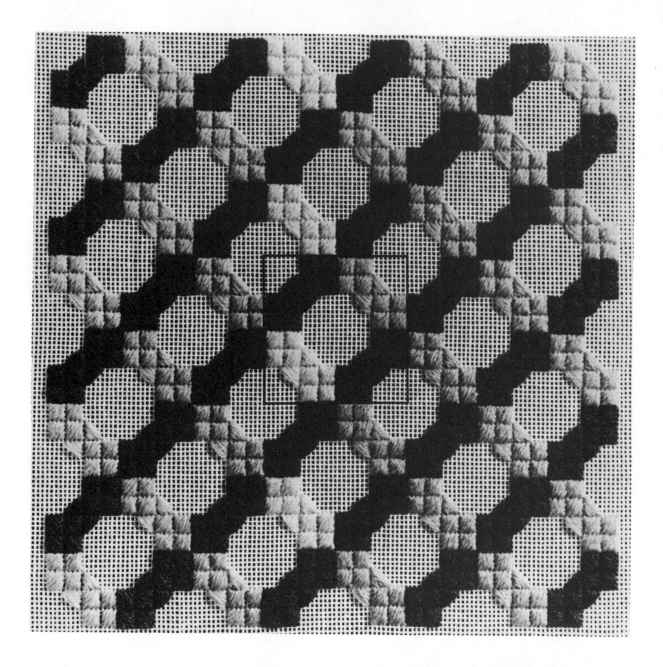

After 1876, quilts were no longer a vital necessity on American beds because industrially woven blankets were inexpensive and readily available. So quilts became objects of decoration, not of necessity. Designs that pictured everyday objects, such as Bow Ties, appeared. The Amish were aware of such worldly changes in styles and reflected them in their plain and simple way.

In fact, few worldly Bow Tie quilts reached the height of sophistication of this Amish composition from the 1920s. A white background was rare in Amish quilts before 1940. Before that time, white was usually worn for funeral clothing.

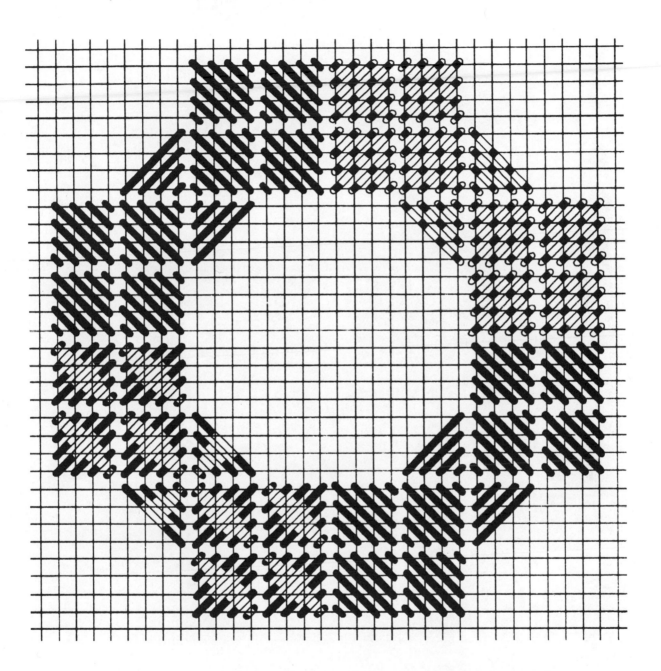

Stitching Directions. Stitch 4 bow ties in the center of the canvas as diagramed. Continue adding bow ties. Note that the dark ties form diagonal stripes and that the light ties of each color form vertical rows. The recommended background stitch is basketweave (#4). The finished piece measures 10″ square on #14 canvas.

Barn Raising

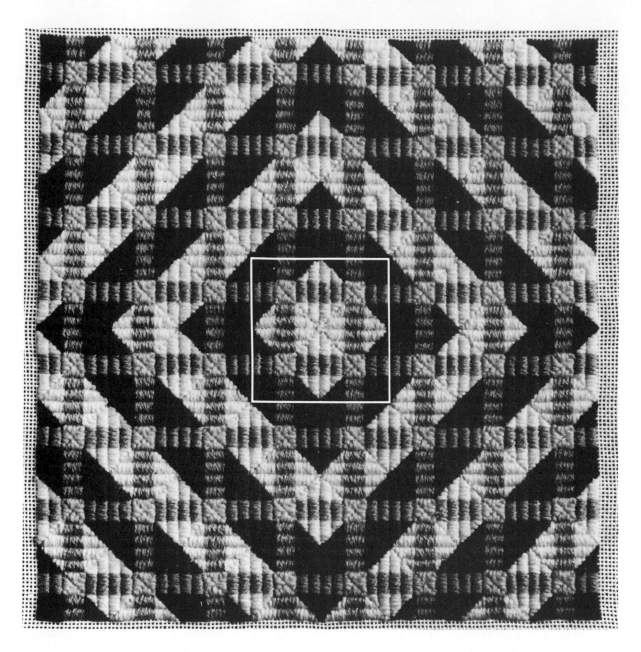

Log Cabin patterns were very popular throughout the United States. Many variations were stitched, including this pattern of concentric diamonds called Barn Raising.

When the Amish used this pattern, they added a simple grid, forming a complex optical illusion. It is as if one is looking at the diamonds through the grid, as through windowpanes. This is a design with great depth.

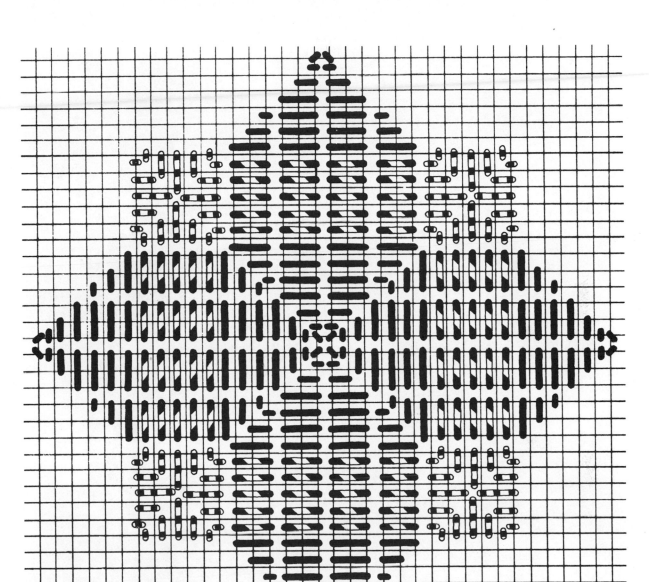

Stitching Directions. Begin in the middle of the canvas, and work central diamond (#1) as diagramed. It is composed of 4 segments worked in alternating directions. The entire piece is composed of these segments. Work the central diamond (#1) in color A and its grid in color B. The next larger diamond (#2-dark) is stitched in color C and its grid in color D. All grid intersections are squares worked in the fifth color, E. Continue alternating light and dark diamonds. The finished piece measures 11″ square on #14 canvas.

Lover's Knot

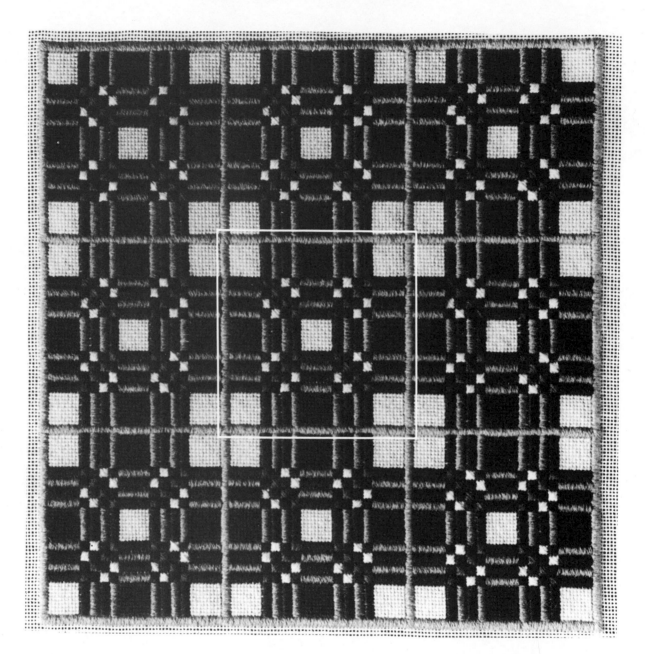

This quilt pattern has no name that we know of. However, it so closely resembles a woven coverlet design named Lover's Knot that one might suppose the coverlet was the inspiration for the quilt. This quilt was stitched in the early part of the twentieth century.

Woven coverlets of such simple designs were produced on home looms for hundreds of years, beginning as early as the seventeenth century. Coverlet names vary as widely and for the same reasons as quilt names.

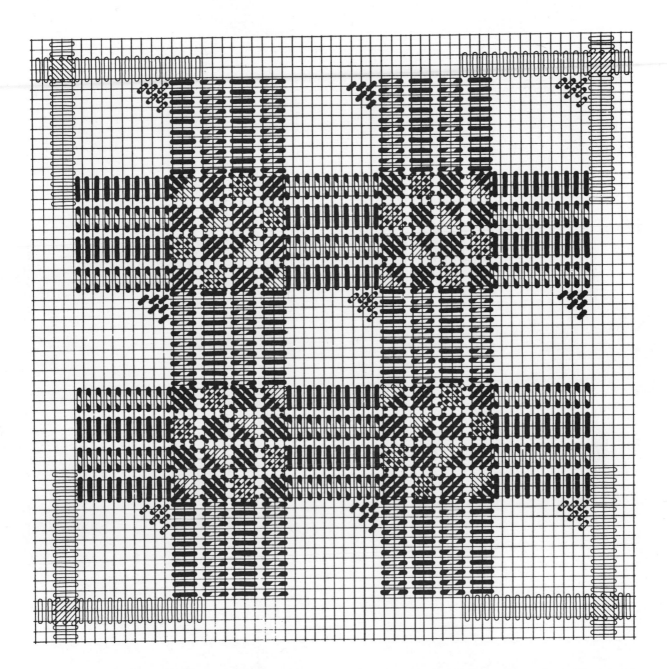

Stitching Directions. Begin stitching this pattern in the center of the canvas. Work as diagramed, stitching basketweave background last. The finished piece measures 12″ square on #14 canvas.

Coverlets

When the first European settlers reached the coast of North America, they brought with them a tradition of woven woolen bedcovers that was already 300 years old. These were called *coverlids, coverlaids,* and many variations in between (spelling was not a strong point with our ancestors). Regardless of how their name was spelled, woven coverlets were a welcome spot of color in early American homes and were highly prized.

As soon as the new settlers could shear sheep and build looms, they began weaving their own coverlets. Before 1725, these were often half wool, half linen (sometimes called *linsey-woolsey*). All yarns were homegrown, homespun, and home dyed, for families had to be self-sufficient. The simple looms available to the colonists limited the designs that they could produce. Such non-pictorial patterns as Lover's Knot were termed *overshot* and were completely geometric. Woven coverlets were most popular in the country, far from commercial centers. Rapid changes of style did not affect country weavers, and overshot patterns changed little over the years.

Many pounds of linen thread or wool yarn were needed to warp a loom. A woman might walk up to twenty miles a day while spinning on a large spinning wheel. Not surprisingly, these were called *walking wheels.*

No housewife could spend all her time spinning, for housekeeping and raising children kept her busy. It usually fell to the older and younger unmarried females in the household to do the bulk of the spinning, and they were therefore called *spinsters.* It took eight full-time spinsters to keep up with one full-time weaver.

Because of the physical strength needed to operate the looms, the men in the family were often the weavers. They farmed in good weather and wove during "odd spells and rainy seasons." Many immigrant weavers who were without homesteads of their own took to the roads as itinerant weavers in the eighteenth century. They were welcome in isolated farmhouses, for they brought news and gossip from the outside world. A weaver wove the family's homespun yarns into cloth on their home loom, which was originally set up in the main living area. However, a housewife got the loom out of her kitchen as soon as she could because the loud weaving noises got on her nerves. Climate had a strong influence on architecture, so looms were moved to upstairs garrets in cold climates but to farm outbuildings in the warmer South.

After the Revolutionary War, Americans moved west over the Appalachians, and new settlements grew and expanded. The Industrial Revolution arrived, and after 1800, cotton thread was spun commercially in New England. Most American housewives stopped spinning flax for their coverlets and bought cotton thread instead. But they still spun and dyed their woolen yarns.

In the nineteenth century, weavers stopped wandering and settled down. Homespun yarns were brought to a professional weaver's loom to be woven into coverlets, and the household loom began to disappear. Some weavers were also dyers, and they would provide that service for an additional fee.

In Indiana from 1800 to 1825, unimproved grazing land sold for $2.50 per acre, and a skilled blacksmith could make $1.50 per day. An experienced weaver could weave an entire coverlet in two days and charge $5.00 for it. Weavers were thus comparatively well paid, and many became prosperous landowners. It was a very respectable trade.

In 1805, a Frenchman named Jacquard perfected a mechanism that was to revolutionize the look of America's coverlets. The Jacquard attachment was an involved system of hooks and pullies that could be added to any loom. Punch cards, the forerunners of those that direct today's computers, controlled pattern production. With the addition of a Jacquard attachment, the simple American loom could produce any pattern, no matter how complex or curving.

The look of these intricate coverlets was very different from that of American quilts of the same period. The differences constitute a before-and-after picture of the Industrial Revolution. Quilts were still made by hand, and the dictates of their construction preserved their essential simplicity. Coverlets were both a product of the new machine age and a realistic picture of it. America was in transition. Suddenly, machines could do what no man had ever done, and new machines were being invented all the time. The sky was the limit. This was a period of intense pride in America's accomplishments and overwhelming optimism for its future. Nothing illustrates this better than the Jacquard coverlets of the period. The new loom gave weavers free reign. In the hands of such masters as Henry Tyler, the results were magnificent. American eagles, portraits of George Washington, and pictures of the Capitol were often woven into their coverlets.

But it was in the coverlet borders that the American weaver really let himself go. Borders were often originated by the weaver. Cards were punched on the spur of the moment to satisfy a customer's whim. Roosters stared at stylish churches, and the most modern of steam engines puffed past village greens. Coverlet borders give us a glimpse of the American scene as it looked more than 150 years ago.

Corner blocks were placed where borders met. These blocks might contain the name of the weaver or that of his customer, the date, or the weaver's personal symbol, such as Harry Tyler's lion. Some corner blocks even contained poems, usually pious or funereal in tone.

During the first half of the nineteenth century, the demand for Jacquard coverlets was constant, and business was good. Families had many children, and an appropriate gift for an engaged son or daughter was a new coverlet. There are records of some families ordering twelve to sixteen coverlets from the same weaver.

But the end of an era was in sight. When the Civil War began, all available wool was needed for army use, and fancy weaving almost stopped between 1861 and 1865. When the war was over, the soldier-weavers came home to find that styles had changed and that their coverlets were no longer in demand. By 1871, Henry La Tourette, a member of the famous Indiana weaving family, finished what was to be his last coverlet. According to his nephew, he "took out his knife, ripped out a great oath, cut the strings, and said, 'This is the end.'" It was.

Handwoven Jacquard coverlets will never be produced in any quantities again, but the freshness and charm of their designs appeal to us today as much as they did to our ancestors. It is a fairy-tale world in which lions look like Yale bulldogs and full-rigged frigates skim over endless seas in search of adventure.

STITCHING INFORMATION

The special charm of these coverlet patterns lies in their simplicity. It is possible to work the designs in this section on either needlepoint canvas or evenweave fabric. We feel that the solid patterns are more easily worked on canvas, with a basketweave background. The open designs will lend themselves well to embroidery on evenweave cloth.

The center of each design is indicated by an *0* on the diagram.

All coverlet patterns in this section can be stitched in any of the three scales described in the Stitching Directions for the first design, Dog. The photographed samples have been stitched in one of these sizes. The remaining two scales are given at the end of the directions for each pattern.

Another method of enlarging or reducing a pattern is to change the gauge of the cloth or canvas on which you work. To determine how altering the gauge will change the size of the finished piece, consult the Canvas Conversion Chart (page 206).

Dog

We have stitched this design in various ways to indicate the differences in finished sizes made possible by the choice of stitches.

The smallest dog is worked in a cross stitch over 1 thread of the canvas. Basketweave could also be used, but there would be a slight loss in the pattern's crispness. This dog is 1⅝″ long when worked on #14 canvas.

The medium-sized dog is stitched in cross stitch over 2 threads of the canvas.

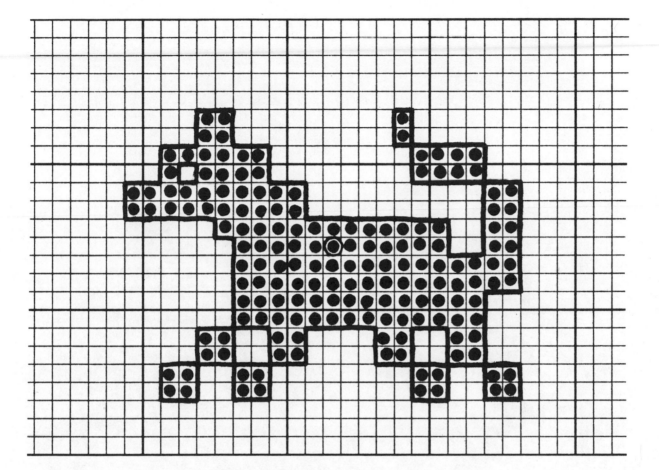

The long-armed cross could be substituted to produce a horizontal effect while maintaining the same size. This dog is 3½″ long when worked on #14 canvas.

The large dog is stitched in a Smyrna cross over 4 threads of the canvas. The flat stitch or the rice stitch could be substituted to produce different textures. This dog is 6½″ long when worked on #14 canvas.

Frigate

"Oh, East is East, and West is West, and never the twain shall meet." Rudyard Kipling was wrong. This frigate was part of a pattern called Christian and Heathen. It mixed palm trees and pagodas with neat New England houses and churches; small sailboats mingled with Chinese junks; steamboats puffed clouds of steam into the air as their waterwheels revolved; and frigates such as this one sailed regally by. The coverlet was woven about 1840. Its colors were the blue of wool dyed with indigo and the natural white of the cotton.

Stitching Directions. The frigate's sails were worked in cross stitch (#10) over 2 threads; the masts and flags, in cross stitch over 1 thread; and the hull, in long-armed cross (#19). Frigate could also be worked totally in cross stitch over 2 threads and still retain the same dimensions. Position the center of the design at the center of the canvas, and work in the stitch of your choice. The straight Milanese (#23) or bargello (#3) would produce a wavelike effect under the ship. The background is stitched in basketweave. The finished piece measures 6″ × 9″ on #14 canvas.

Over 1 thread, 3″ × 4½″.

Over 4 threads, 12″ × 18″.

Engine and Train

This early passenger train was the trademark of the weaver Peter Grimm of Loudonville, Ohio, who first stitched it in 1857. Two layers of trains formed the side borders of his coverlets, enclosing medallions of overblown roses and gigantic tuliplike flowers. Borders that we would consider wildly out of step

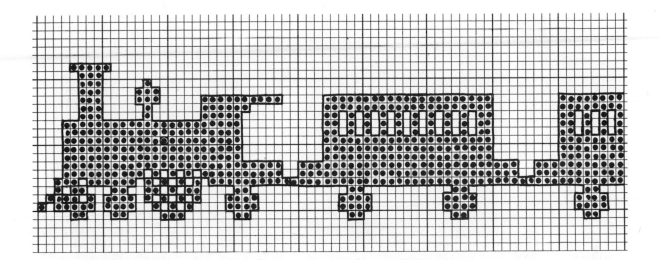

with the central motif were often used with happy abandon.

The first locomotive used in America was called the *Tom Thumb* and was built in 1829. But the one pictured here has a larger driving wheel on its side, a new invention in 1850. It was the latest word in locomotives when this coverlet was woven. The cowcatcher firmly attached to the front of the locomotive reminds us of the vast unfenced spaces that trains such as this opened to civilization.

Stitching Directions. This train is worked on evenweave fabric with a cross stitch over 2 threads. Work the engine as diagramed, and add as many cars as you wish. When Train is used for a belt or border, have one train pointing left attached to an identical train pointing right, in the center back (page 186). The finished piece measures 3″ × 12″ when worked on evenweave fabric with 16 threads per inch.

Over 1 thread, 1½″ × 6″.
Over 4 threads, 6″ × 24″.

This engine is the same as that used in Train and Engine. It is worked in a Smyrna cross (#29) over 4 threads. The finished piece measures 7″ × 4″ when worked on evenweave fabric with 8 threads per inch.

Over 1 thread, 1¾″ x 1″.
Over 2 threads, 3½″ x 2″.

Lion

This lion was the symbol or trademark of Harry Tyler, a weaver from Jefferson County, New York. Tyler, a draftsman of exceptional ability, began weaving in 1834 and continued for twenty-four years.

The best spinner in the neighborhood took great pride in producing smooth thread for Tyler coverlets. Tyler dyed the wool himself in a large brass pot. Tyler's sons had the weekly chore of cleaning and polishing the dye pot with old brooms and a mixture of salt and vinegar. Tyler charged $2.75 for weaving one coverlet or $2.50 each if the order was for more than one of the same weave.

Coverlet weavers often drew their

own patterns and then transferred them to the cards that directed the Jacquard looms. These cards were punched by hand and were the forerunners of today's computer punch cards.

Stitching Directions. The face and mane of the lion have been worked in a cross stitch over 1 thread. The remainder of his body was worked in basketweave (#4). Position the center of the design at the center of the canvas, and stitch as diagramed. The original coverlet from which this pattern was taken showed the year 1839 beneath the tip of the lion's tail. That would be a good place to stitch your initials. Use a contrasting color for the basketweave background. The finished piece measures 6″ × 7″ when worked on #14 canvas.

Over 2 threads, 12″ x 14″.
Over 4 threads, 24″ x 28″.

Village Green

This rose tree with its picket fence border was woven by Harry Tyler in 1839. Today, we think of picket fences as white, but the American delight in white paint dates from the Greek revival period, when interest in classical antiquities was at its height. White dresses, white wood carvings, and white buildings were meant to simulate classical marble. But the picket fences surrounding earlier village greens were painted a darker color or left unpainted.

The village green of an early New England town was used to pasture the townspeople's sheep, and the town selectmen were required to keep the land clear for grazing.

Stitching Directions. Work the border as diagramed on page 188. Dotted stitches indicate a cross stitch over 1 thread. Open areas indicate the long-armed cross over 2 or 3 threads. The tree is stitched in a cross stitch over 1 thread. Position the center of the tree at the center of cloth or canvas. Work the trunk and branches of the tree. Then stitch the leaves and fruit. Place the man and dog beneath the tree as diagramed, and stitch them in cross stitch over 1 thread. The suggested needlepoint background stitch is basketweave (#4). This pattern would also work well on evenweave fabric. The finished piece measures 11″ square on #14 canvas.

Over 2 threads, 22″ square.
Over 4 threads, 44″ square.

Blue Birds

Pairs of birds often perch on woven coverlet borders. They could well serve as lovebirds. This coverlet was woven in Clinton County, Ohio, in 1839. Its colors were indigo blue and natural cotton.

Stitching Directions. First work the leaf stitch border as diagramed on page 189. Corner leaves are 1 thread apart; they do not touch. Surround the leaves with the long-armed cross (#19). Position the birds equally on either side of the center of the canvas, and stitch as diagramed. The birds were stitched in

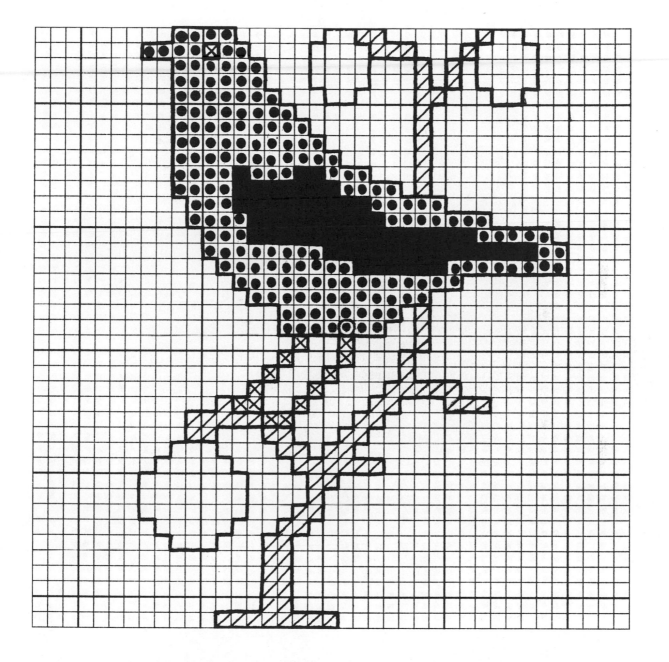

long-armed cross, and the remainder of the pattern is in cross stitch over 2 threads. The design could be stitched entirely in a cross stitch over 2 threads without changing the dimensions. The suggested needlepoint background is basketweave. This pattern would also work well on evenweave fabric. The finished piece measures 9″ × 12″ on #14 canvas.

Over 1 thread, 4½″ x 6″.
Over 4 threads, 18″ x 24″.

Rooster

Woven coverlets reached the height of their popularity far from the large cities, where styles changed rapidly. Coverlet weavers often designed borders to suit the whim of a particular customer. In view of the fact that many of these customers were farmers, it is not surprising that barnyard inhabitants often appear in the borders of woven coverlets. This jaunty rooster graced a coverlet woven in 1834 by David D. Haring, of Bergen County, New Jersey. Its colors were those of natural linen and indigo-dyed wool. Linen was rarely used to weave coverlets in the 1830s because by then industrially spun cotton was readily available.

Stitching Directions. The details of this pattern were stitched in a cross stitch over 1 thread. The remainder of the bird was worked in basketweave. Position the center of the rooster in the center of the canvas or cloth. Work cross stitch first, then add basketweave. Use a contrasting color for the basketweave background. The finished piece measures 3″ square on #14 canvas.

Over 2 threads, 6″ square.

Over 4 threads, 12″ square.

#

Most of the coverlets illustrated in this section were woven during the intensely patriotic period from 1820 to 1860. The citizens of the small, young Republic were very proud of its aims and accomplishments.

Although Benjamin Franklin had fa-vored the turkey as America's symbol, the eagle finally prevailed. This eagle adorned a coverlet woven by David Haring, of Bergen County, New Jersey, in 1832. It was woven entirely of wool in light and dark blue.

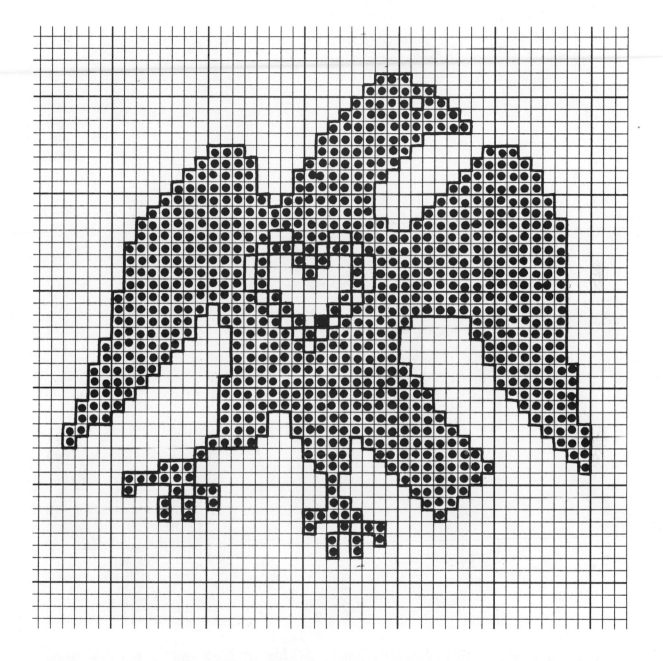

Stitching Directions. The body and details of this eagle were stitched in a cross stitch over 2 threads. Position the center of the eagle in the center of canvas or cloth. Work the bird first and the heart and eye last. The finished piece measures 6″ square on #14 canvas.

Over 1 thread, 3″ square.

Over 4 threads, 12″ square.

Peacock

Lordly manor houses in England had magnificent gardens inhabited by peacocks. Although few peacocks strutted around America's farms, the bird was known to rural Americans, if only through pictures, and was cherished for its color and grace. It was a symbol of luxury. What better motif could be woven into a coverlet, itself a luxury item?

This peacock was the trademark of William Hicks, of Madison County, Indiana. It was woven in 1850 with natural cotton and light blue, dark blue, green, and red wool.

Many coverlets were woven with bands of differing colors crossing horizontally and intersecting the designs where they would. The effect was bright, sparkling, and very decorative,

though far from naturalistic.

Stitching Directions. First work the border as diagramed on page 190. The intersection of lines extending from the center of each heart is the center of the canvas. Position the central motif at this point. The peacock was stitched in a cross stitch over 1 thread. Begin stitching at the center of the pattern. If you wish to work the peacock in three col-

lors, as diagramed, work the center band of color first. The design would also be effective stitched in a single color. The finished piece measures 11″ square on #14 canvas. The peacock alone measures 5½″.

Over 2 threads, 22″ square; peacock, 11″.

Over 4 threads, 44″ square; peacock, 22″.

Paddle Boat

The first American steamboat was the *Clermont,* built by Robert Fulton in 1807. The use of steam power became increasingly widespread, and soon *side wheelers* were crossing the Atlantic Ocean. The steam-powered ships of the time were also equipped with sails. It paid to have both, for neither source of power was totally reliable.

This paddle boat was part of the same coverlet design, Christian and Heathen, that inspired Frigate (page 136). The coverlet shows an odd variety of ships in Canton harbor which seems historically unlikely. But the midwestern weaver of 1840 placed his boats where he wanted them, with happy disregard for the realities of history. His primary concern

was the appearance of his coverlet.

Stitching Directions. This boat was stitched in a cross stitch over 2 threads. Position the center of the boat in the center of the canvas. Stitch the boat as diagramed; then work the smoke. For a watery effect beneath the boat, try the straight Milanese (#23) or bargello (#2). The finished piece measures 7″ x 10″ on #14 canvas.

Over 1 thread, 3½″ x 5″.
Over 4 threads, 17″ x 20″.

Chinese Junk

This Chinese junk sailed between the frigate and the paddle boat in Canton harbor on the same 1840s coverlet. It is doubtful that any coverlet weaver ever actually saw a junk, but he knew what they looked like from books and pictures. The Chinese Chippendale period in America during the late eighteenth century had awakened interest in the Orient. Oriental motifs frequently appeared, appropriately or not, in nineteenth-century America's decorative art.

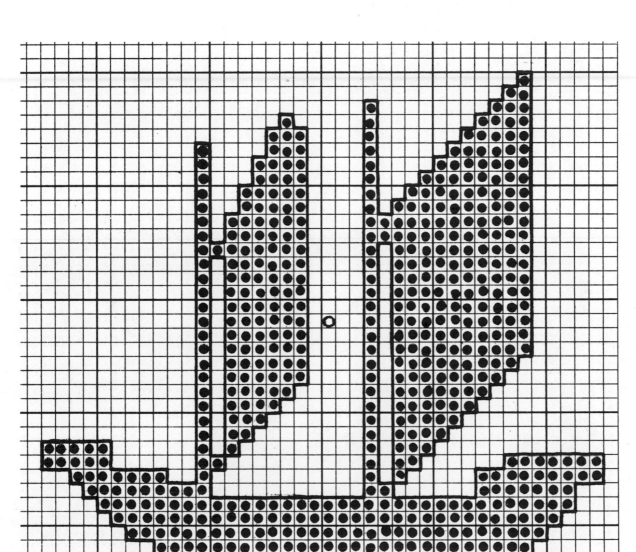

Stitching Directions. This junk was stitched in the long-armed cross. Its sails and masts were worked in cross stitch over 2 threads. Center the pattern in the center of the canvas. Stitch the boat as diagramed. This motif would be equally effective with the boat and masts stitched in one color and the sails stitched in a second color. Straight Milanese (#23) or bargello (#2) would produce a wavelike effect under the junk. The finished piece measures 5″ square on #14 canvas.

Over 1 thread, 2½″ square.
Over 4 threads, 10″ square.

Church

The Gothic revival was all the fashion after 1830, and the church that inspired this design must have been the height of style in the New Jersey of 1832.

The church may have had its cross turned into a weather vane at the insistance of the person who ordered the coverlet. The pointed arches of the

building's windows and door reflect the Gothic style. The roof is patterned with different colored shingles, a very popular style in rural America during the early nineteenth century.

Stitching Directions. This building was stitched in a cross stitch over 1

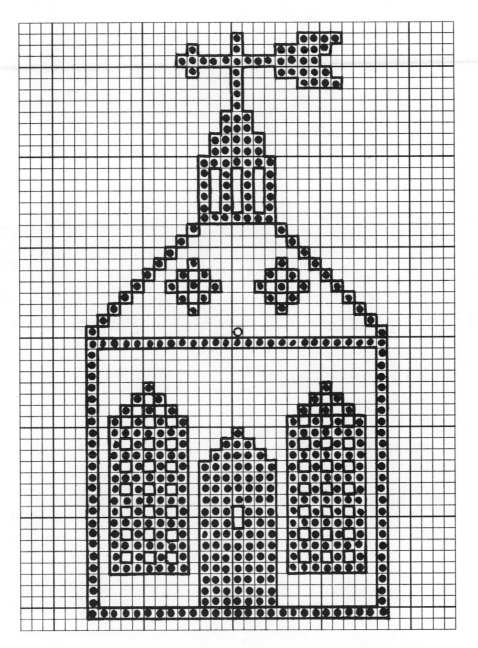

thread. Position the center of the church in the center of the canvas or cloth. Stitch the church as diagramed; then add the windows and the roof design. If a border is desired, work it as diagramed on page 188. The suggested needlepoint stitch for filling in the church is the basketweave (#4) or brick (#5). If the brick stitch is used, the window and roof details should be filled in with basketweave. The recommended background stitch is basketweave. The finished piece measures 4½" square on #14 canvas.

Over 2 threads, 9" square.
Over 4 threads, 18" square.

Samplers

During the Middle Ages, most fine European embroidery was worked by professional embroiderers, many of whom were men, and most needleworks were commissioned by the Church. It was not until the Renaissance, in the sixteenth century, that embroidery began to decorate man instead of God. With this rise in personal ornamentation came a parallel rise in amateur needlework of very fine quality.

Seventeenth-century women had no pattern books to follow. Instead, they stitched memorable designs on long, narrow strips of cloth so that they would have a reminder of how to work various stitches when need arose. These cloth memo pads, called *examplers* or *samplers,* were not displayed; they were rolled and put away until needed for reference.

The first American samplers were of this long, narrow rolled type. They took the place of design books, which were unavailable here, and they were worked by grown women over the age of fifteen. Printed fabrics were almost nonexistent in the colonies during the seventeenth century, and when they could be imported, they were very expensive. When a woman wanted patterned cloth, she had to embroider.

By the middle of the eighteenth century, American samplers changed in function and in shape. Pattern books were published, and grown women no longer needed samplers as stitching guides. Samplers were used as teaching instruments. Girls from five to fifteen learned their numbers and alphabet at home or at school by stitching them on nearly square pieces of fabric. The finished samplers were framed and hung in the best parlor to be admired and handed down to future generations.

During the latter part of the eighteenth century and most of the nineteenth, formal education for young women became more common. Needlework became part of every girl's schooling, and needlework instruction passed from the hands of mothers to those of teachers. Pictures were introduced into samplers, along with poems, hymns, pious sayings, and Bible verses. Needlework was also used as a method of teaching other subjects. Map samplers and family genealogies were stitched by young students.

Not all girls took to this discipline with equal fervor. Their attitudes ranged from that of a girl who stitched, "Mary Dudden were 12 years of age when this Sampler were worked, and some part of it by moonlight," to less happy emotions of a young woman who wrote that she "worked this sampler and hated every stitch she put in it."

By the middle of the nineteenth century, American industry was capable of supplying household linens and clothing for its population. The necessity for sewing decreased, and needlework assumed a less important role in a young woman's education. Samplers were no longer needed as educational tools.

Nevertheless, the original practice of "jotting down" stitches as a reminder of how to work them is as valid as it ever was. This is obvious from the great number of needlepoint samplers worked by today's women. When this form of stitching instruction is combined with designs from patchwork quilt blocks, the result is indeed delightful.

STITCHING INFORMATION

Samplers in this section will allow any needleworker to learn a variety of stitches. Well-designed samplers and well-thought-out stitch directions can help to organize and teach a basic needlepoint class. We use these samplers and directions in our classes at the Henry Ford Museum. We recommend working them with stranded yarn.

To begin, outline the sampler design on canvas, with a waterproof marker in a medium or light color, marking between two continuous threads. (To check the waterproof qualities of a marker, color a scrap of needlepoint canvas, and rub it with a wet cloth. If any ink bleeds onto the cloth, change the brand of marking pen.) Make sure that the appropriate number of *threads* (not holes) lie between the two lines. Stitches cover a particular number of threads, but several stitches can share one hole.

Our students begin by working a row of upright Gobelin stitches around the edge of the sampler. They learn straight stitches first, then cross stitches, then diagonal stitches. The basketweave is the last stitch taught because it fills in the sampler background. A long-armed cross border often encloses the upright Gobelin border. The numbers on the overall sampler diagrams refer to the individual stitch diagrams in the Stitching Guide.

All diagrams are color-coded. The samplers are worked in three tones—dark, medium, and light—in dark and medium combinations, and in medium and light combinations. The tones are diagramed as follows:

DARK   MEDIUM   LIGHT

LIGHT, MEDIUM AND DARK   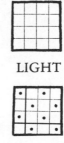 MEDIUM AND DARK   MEDIUM AND LIGHT

These samplers are based upon checkerboard blocks or modules. All modules are square. There are the same number of modules horizontally as vertically. All modules within a given sampler will contain the same number of canvas threads. A sampler with 3 modules per side will contain 9 small squares, each containing equal numbers of threads.

An example is Variable Star.

A sampler with 5 modules per side will contain 25 equal squares, each containing the same number of threads. An example is the Tide Wheel.

All the samplers in this section are worked on #14 canvas. The borders worked around each sampler account for the variations in size.

Maple Leaf

The Maple Leaf was also known as Autumn Leaf. The inspiration for many American quilt patterns came directly from the pastures and forests. Flowers, leaves, and trees were familiar shapes that could be traced or copied to make quilt patterns.

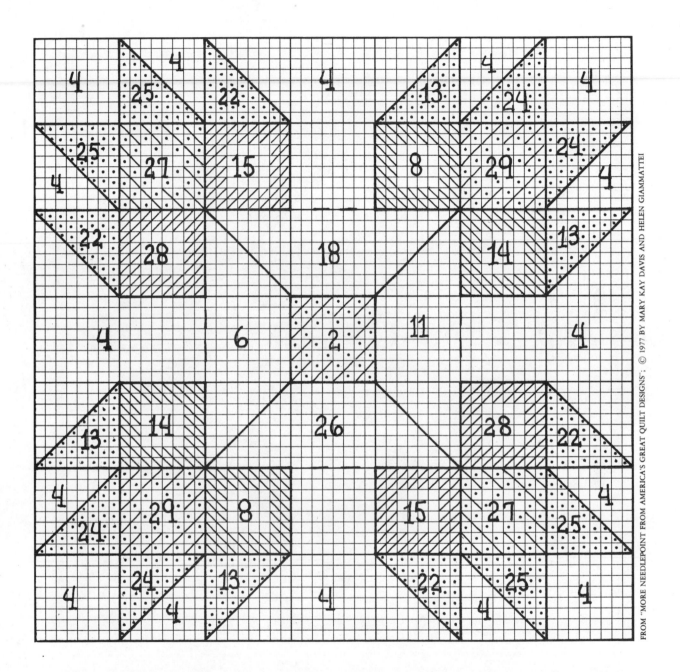

Stitching Directions. This sampler includes seventeen stitches plus upright Gobelin (#16) and long-armed cross (#19) borders. There are 7 modules per side of 16 threads each, for a total of 112 threads. The piece measures 9½″ square on #14 canvas. The rice stitch is worked in a dark tone for the large X on bottom and in a medium tone for the crossed corners. The Smyrna cross is worked in a dark tone for the bottom X and in a medium tone for the top cross. The leaf stems may be worked in diagonal long-armed cross (#20) before the adjacent areas are stitched or in backstitch (#1) after the adjacent areas have been completed.

Friendship Squares

This is an example of a block from a friendship or album quilt. The purpose of the nineteenth-century friendship quilting bee was to assemble a wedding quilt or to give a gift to a dear friend who was moving away. Each guest brought a signed quilt block. These were joined together to form the top. The quilting of the top was done later.

Album quilt blocks were often signed with the name of the stitcher. If poems were stitched on the quilt block, they were usually of a sentimental nature, and the finished quilt was called a *remembrance quilt*. When biblical quotations were used, the quilt was called a *Bible quilt*. Such a quilt was considered especially appropriate as a gift for a

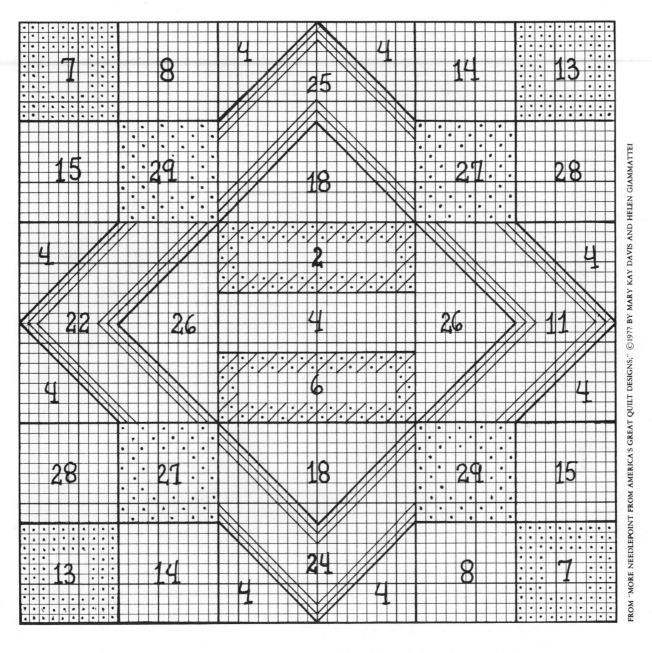

minister who was moving to another parish.

Stitching Directions. This sampler includes seventeen stitches plus upright Gobelin (#16) and long-armed cross (#19) borders. The Rice stitch is worked in a medium tone for large X on the bottom and in a light ton t the crossed corners. The Smyrna cross is worked in a medium tone for the bottom X and in a light tone for the top cross. There are 6 modules per side of 20 threads each, for a total of 120 threads. The piece measures 10″ square on #14 canvas.

Chain Link

Chain Link is a variation of an older pattern called Strips and Squares. Iron chains were usually made by the local blacksmith. He would put two or three wrought iron rods into his fire and heat them until they turned cherry red. He would withdraw one rod, cut off enough iron for one link, and bend it on the anvil with a few blows of his hammer. The U-shaped link would then be hooked through the preceding link of the chain and welded closed. Expert blacksmiths could forge two yards of chain per hour at a rate of one link per minute. Such a blacksmith in Indiana earned $1.50 a day in 1825.

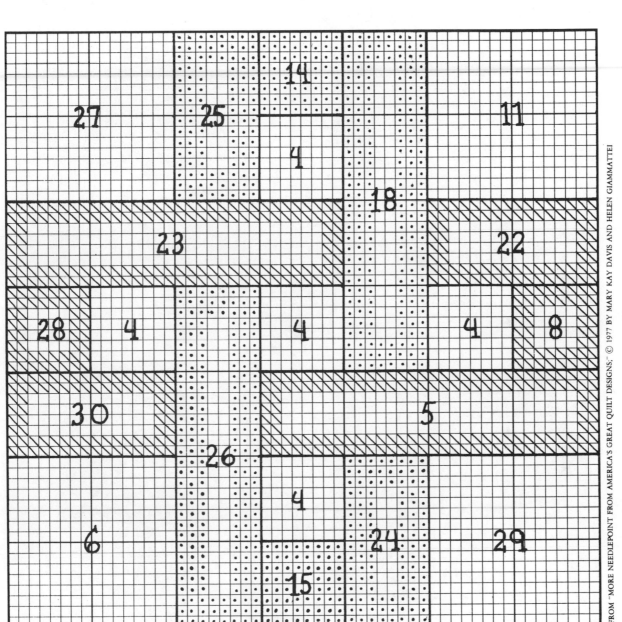

Stitching Directions. This sampler includes seventeen stitches plus a border worked in long-armed cross (#19). There are 7 modules per side of 16 threads each, for a total of 112 threads.

The piece measures 9″ square on #14 canvas.

City Streets

The majority of nineteenth-century Americans were rural farmers and small-town folk. A visit to a large, bustling city must have been an unforgettable experience for them. City Streets—with its central square, main streets, and separate neighborhoods—could be a logical plan for a town.

Stitching Directions. This sampler includes eighteen stitches and an upright Gobelin (#16) border. There are 7 modules per side of 16 threads each, for a total of 112 threads. Work the center

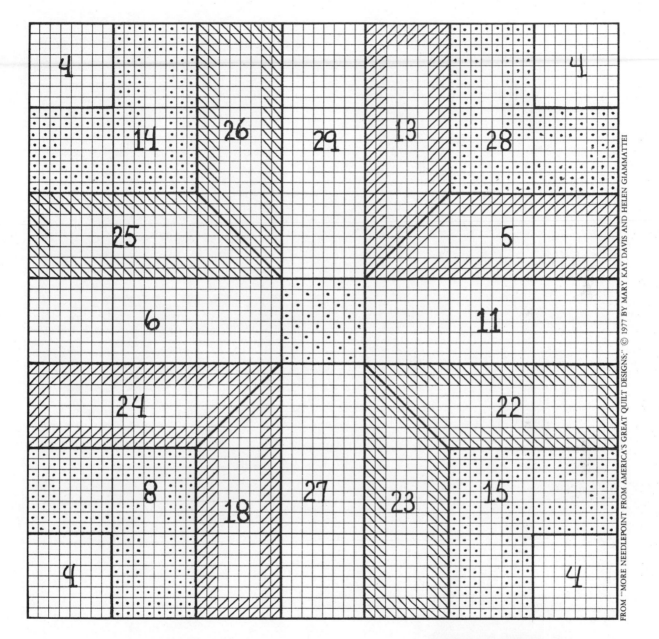

motif as diagramed. After the dark sections are completed, miter lines are overstitched with the backstitch (#1). The piece measures 9″ square on #14 canvas.

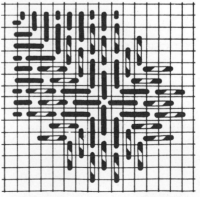

Tide Wheel

Tide Wheel is also known as Mill Wheel, Crown of Thorns, Georgetown Circle, and Memory Wreath. The pattern of a Memory Wreath quilt was cut from pieces of the departed's clothing, and the date of death and name were embroidered in the center square.

Tide Wheels were used to power early mills along the Atlantic Coast. High tides filled the millpond. The tide pushed the water through a tide race, to the mill and its wheels. The seawater

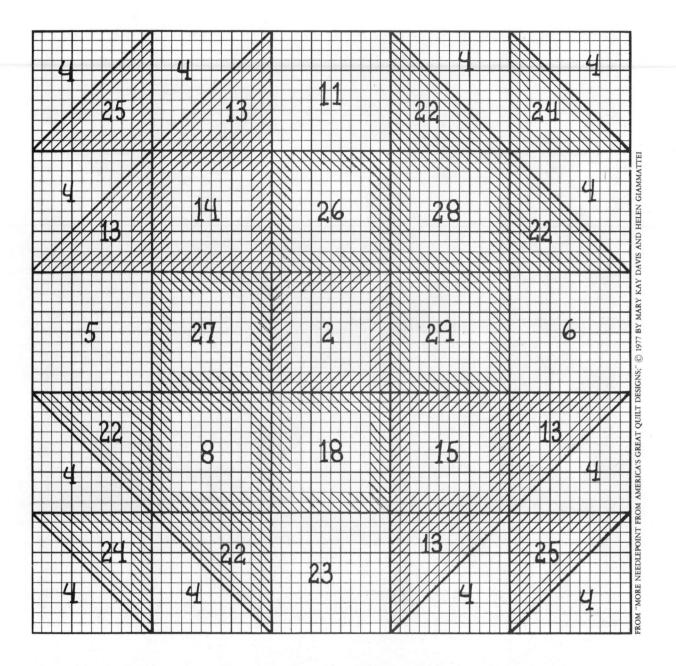

turned the wheels until the tide went out and the millpond was empty; then all work ceased until the next high tide.

Stitching Directions. This sampler includes eighteen stitches plus an up-right Gobelin (#16) border. There are 5 modules per side of 24 threads each, for a total of 120 threads. This sampler is worked in two tones, light and dark. The piece measures 10″ square on #14 canvas.

New Mexico

New Mexico is also called Three Crosses, Golgotha, and Cross upon Cross. It is a slight variation of the Cross and Crown of colonial days.

The state of New Mexico, a U.S. territory since 1850, was admitted to the Union in 1912. At the time this quilt pattern originated, New Mexico was famous for its Sante Fe Trial, which opened in the early nineteenth century and closed when the Atchison, Topeka, and Santa Fe Railroad was completed in 1880.

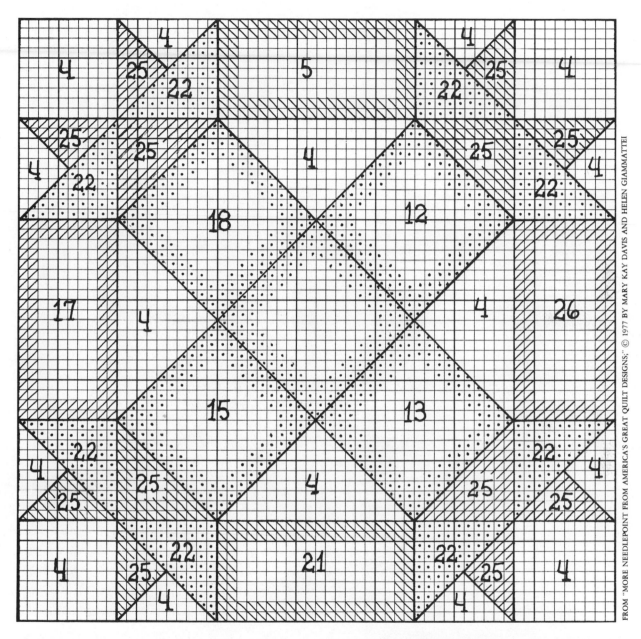

Stitching Directions. This sampler includes 12 stitches and a long-armed cross (#19) border. There are 6 modules per side of 20 threads each, for a total of 120 threads. Work the center bargello diamond as diagramed. The piece measures 9½" square on #14 canvas.

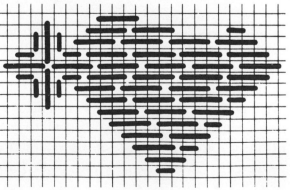

Duck Paddle

Duck Paddle is a slight variation of Goose Tracks, which is a variation of Bear Paw. Bear Tracks is the oldest version of this design. In rural areas, the muddy tracks of animals, both wild and barnyard, were common. Bears began moving out when farms and settlements moved in. The next generation of quil-ters may never have seen a bear's tracks, but they were thoroughly familiar with ducks.

Stitching Directions. This sampler includes twenty stitches. As diagramed, there are 5 modules per side of 24 threads each, for a total of 120 threads,

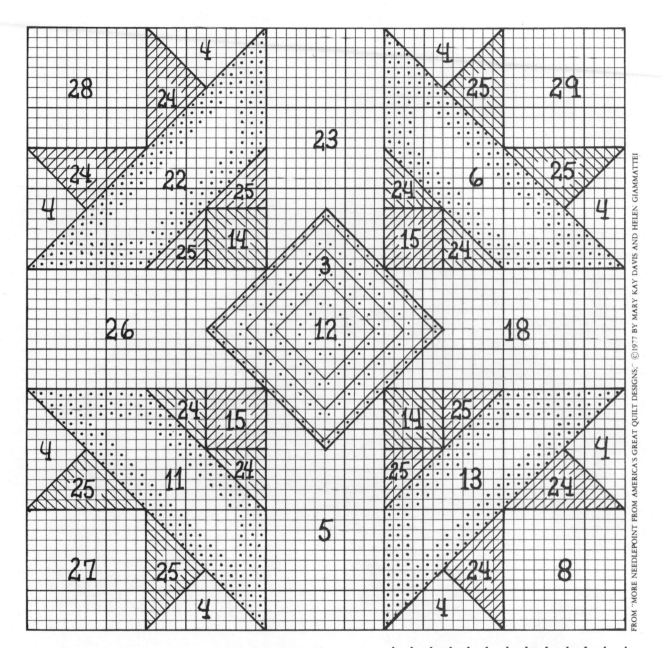

measuring 9″ square on #14 canvas. The photographed sampler has been enlarged. Each of the 5 modules contains 36 threads, instead of 24, enlarging the sampler by 50 percent. The finished piece, as photographed, measures 14″ square on #14 canvas.

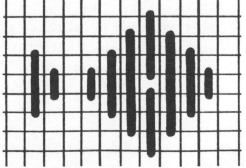

Variable Star

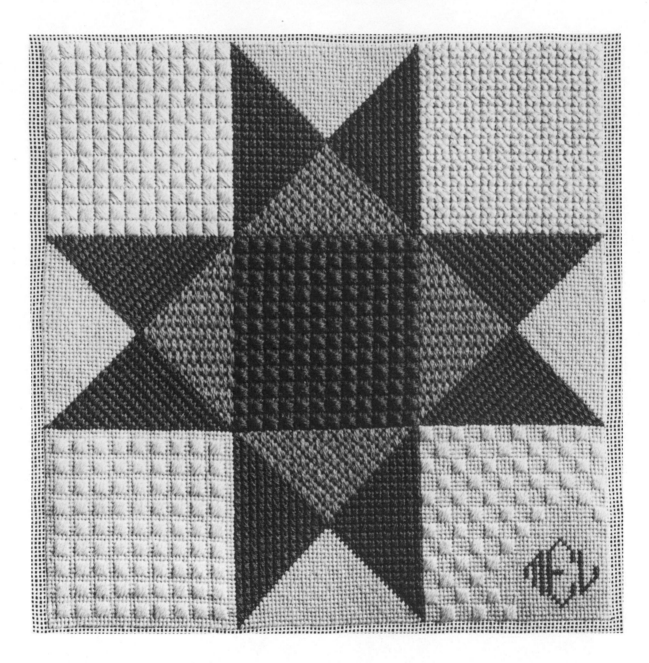

This pattern was called Variable Star in the early nineteenth century. When Texas became a state in 1845, this popular star pattern was renamed the Texas Star. It was also called the Lone Star.

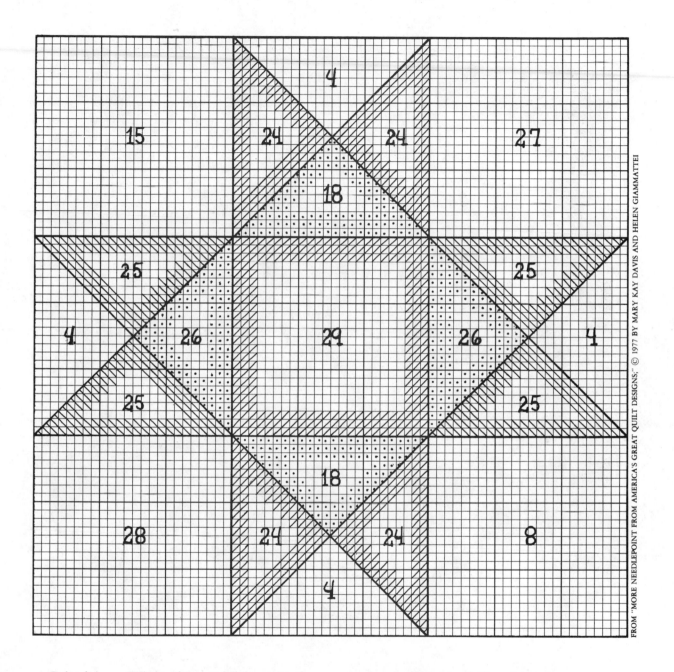

Stitching Directions. This sampler includes ten stitches. There are 3 modules per side of 48 threads each, for a total of 144 threads. The piece measures 11″ square on #14 canvas.

Mosaic

Most mosaic quilts are composed of hexagons. Yet this pattern, which dates from the last years of the nineteenth century, more closely resembles another early design called Lazy Daisy or Cupid's Arrowpoint.

Few colonial or early American homes had stone or tile mosaic floors. But pieced quilts, cut and carefully arranged to produce many of the same compositions used in such floors, were mosaics of gentler materials.

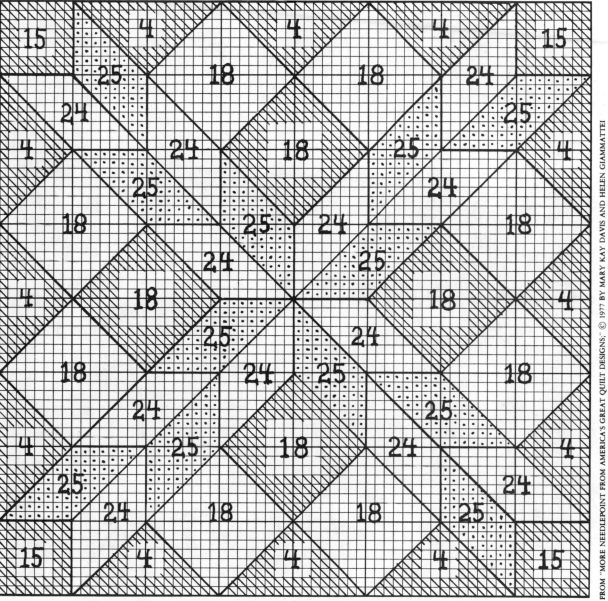

Stitching Directions. This sampler includes five stitches. There are 8 modules per side of 8 threads each, for a total of 64 threads. Unlike the samplers on the previous pages, which are worked in a ratio of 2 stitches to 1 square on the overall diagram, this one is stitched in the same scale as the diagram. The piece measures 5″ square on #14 canvas.

Whirligig

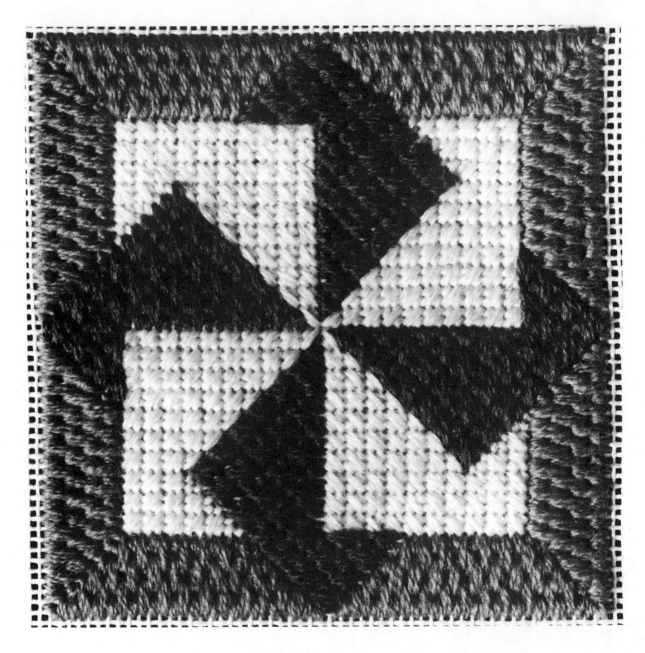

A whirligig, an eighteenth-century toy with paddlelike arms, was meant to be set up outdoors, where the arms would be whirled around by the wind. In a time when toys were few and often handmade, the whirligig must have provided pleasure for child and adult alike. The Whirligig sampler is based on one stitch, the Hungarian, and its diagonal variation, the mosaic.

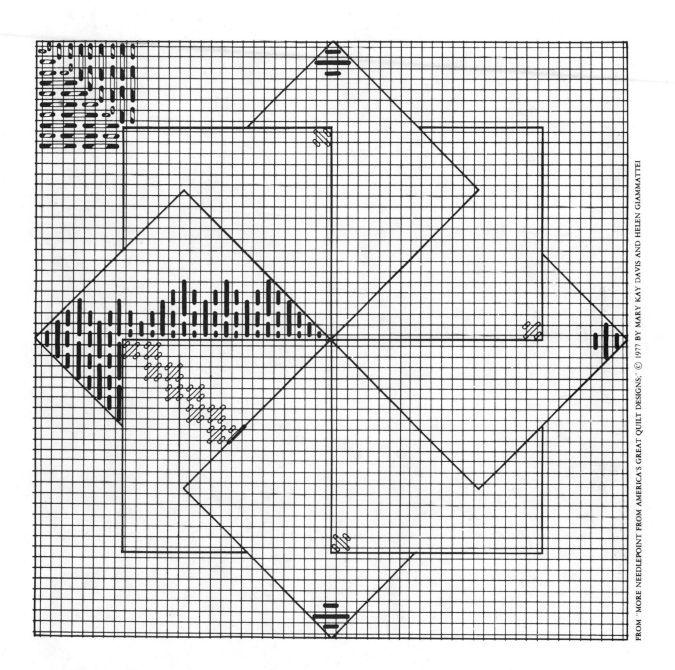

Stitching Directions. This sampler is not composed of modules. Each side measures 56 threads. Stitch the dark arms of the whirligig as diagramed. Then work the light arms that form the inner square. Stitch the brick border, as diagramed, last. The finished piece measures 4″ square on #14 canvas.

Initial

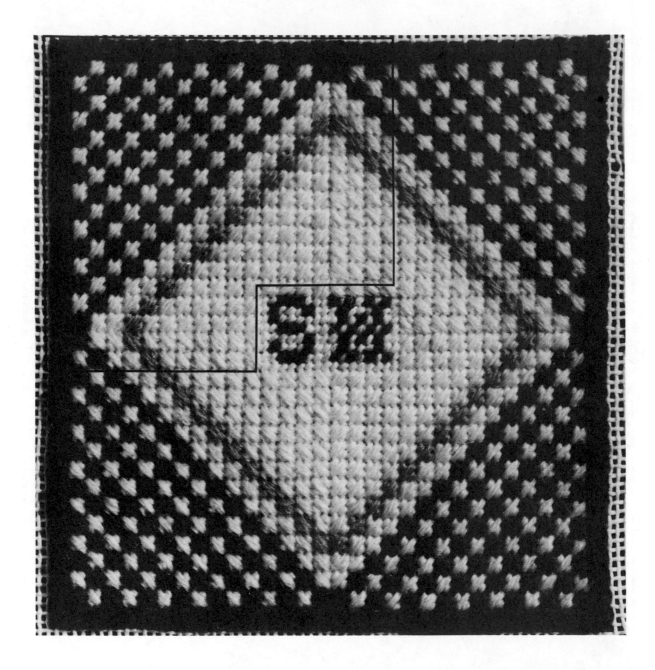

The initial sampler explores the design possibilities of one stitch, the mosaic. It could easily be enlarged by substituting a flat, Smyrna cross, or rice stitch for each square.

The initials are worked in a traditional cross stitch alphabet that was widely used during the eighteenth and nineteenth centuries. Sometimes, quilts were pieced with small patches that formed the letters of biblical quotations or individual names. In most cases these quilt letters follow the form of this cross stitch alphabet.

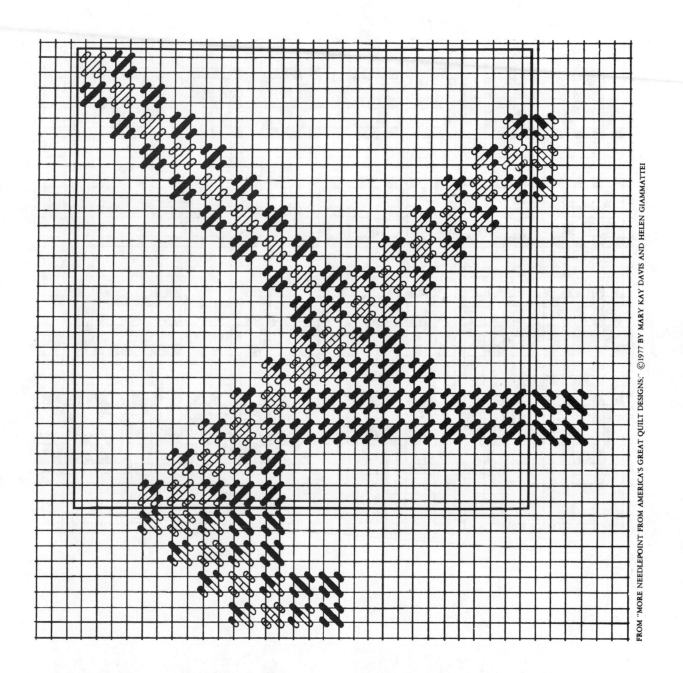

Stitching Directions. Each side contains 60 threads. Stitch the sampler as diagramed, working diagonally from each corner toward the center. Note that the slant of each quadrant is different. Complete mosaic stitches. The monogram is worked within an oblong, stitched in basketweave, that is 8 threads high and as wide as necessary. Each letter covers 7 vertical threads. (See Initial Alphabet, page 184.) The eighth row of basketweave stitches is worked below the initials. Work initials in cross stitch over 1 thread of the canvas. The finished piece measures 5″ square on #14 canvas.

See alphabet on page 184.

Alphabet

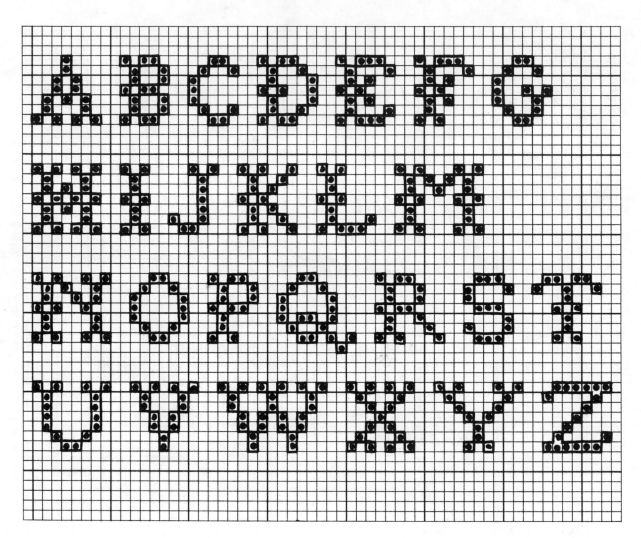

Belts
and Borders

Boat, Spool, Bow Tie, Ribbon, Cable & Train

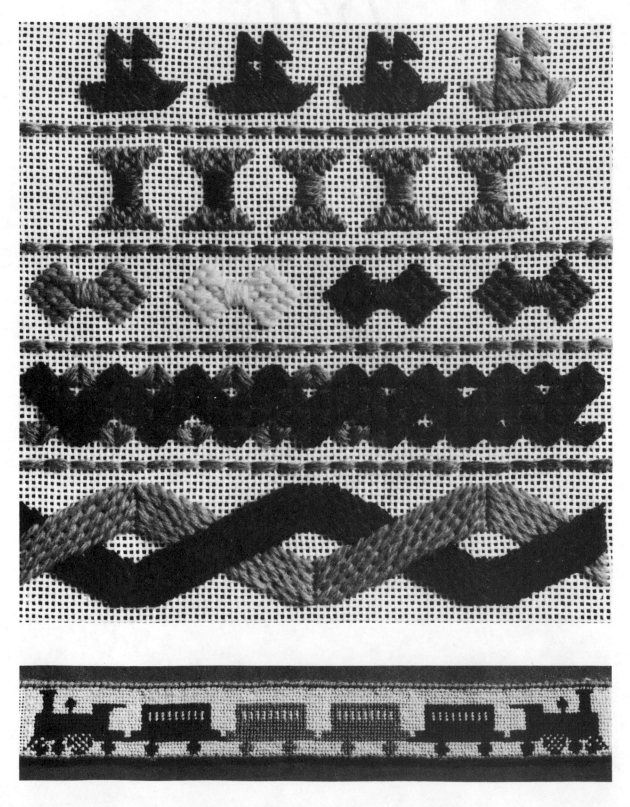

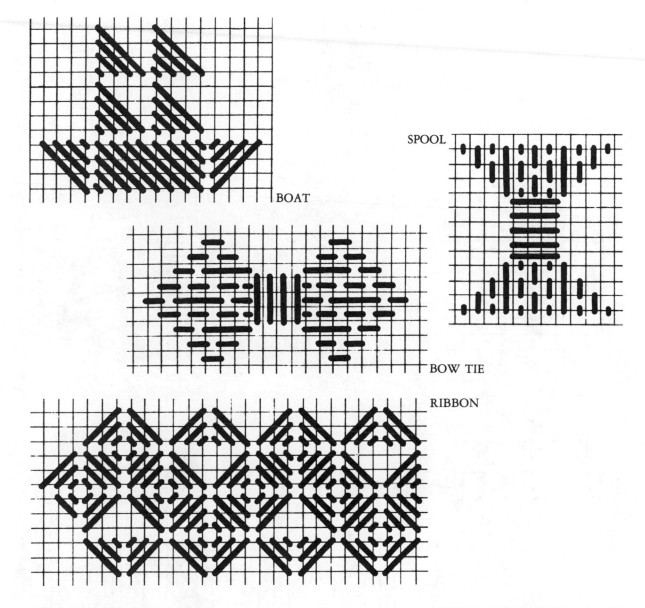

BOAT

SPOOL

BOW TIE

RIBBON

CABLE BORDER *See page 105*

ENGINE AND TRAIN *See page 139*

Borders serve the same function in needlepoint as they did in quilting: They frame and enlarge the pattern within them.

The designs in this section are effective on belts. Corner blocks, with initials or dates, would be necessary to make some of them turn corners. Stitch the designs as diagramed.

Some borders, such as Sunshine and Shadow, Blue Birds, Church, and Spring Garden, have small modules and are easily expanded. Other borders, such as Peacock and Village Green, are composed of much larger modules. These frames should be worked first. The pictures they contain should be centered and stitched last.

Village Green & Church

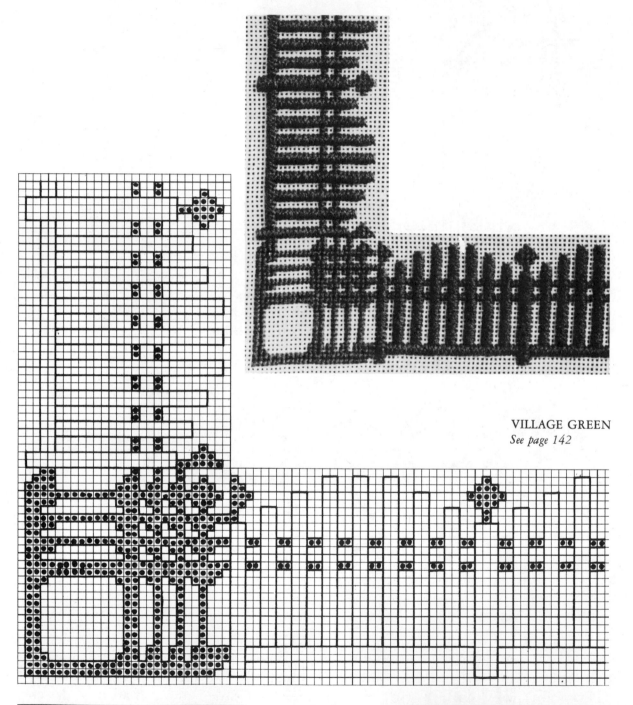

VILLAGE GREEN
See page 142

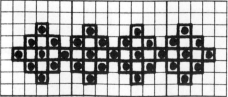

CHURCH
See page 156

Sunshine and Shadow
Blue Birds & Spring Garden

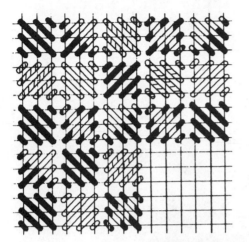

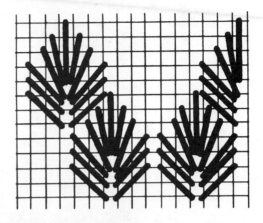

BLUE BIRDS
See page 144

**SUNSHINE
AND
SHADOW**
See page 112

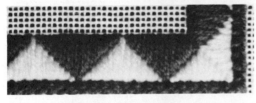

SPRING GARDEN
See page 46

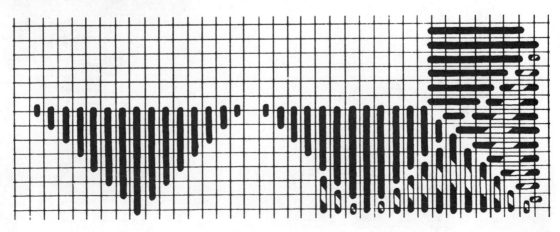

Peacock

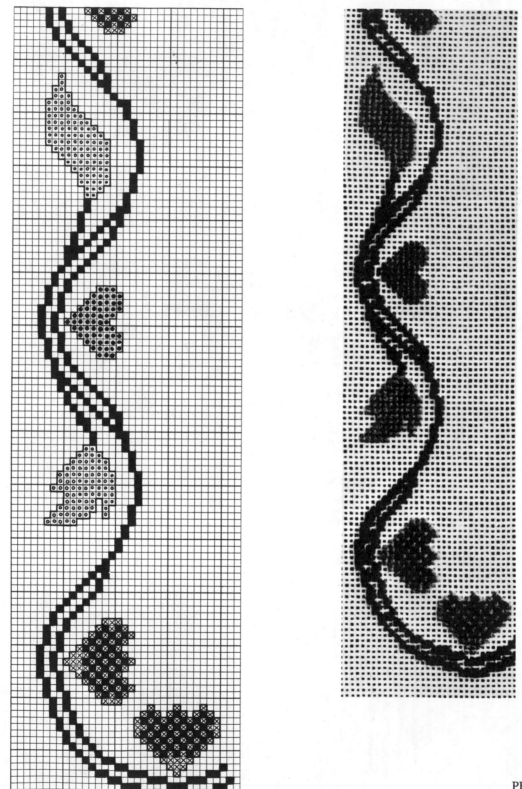

PEACOCK
See page 150

Pine Cone

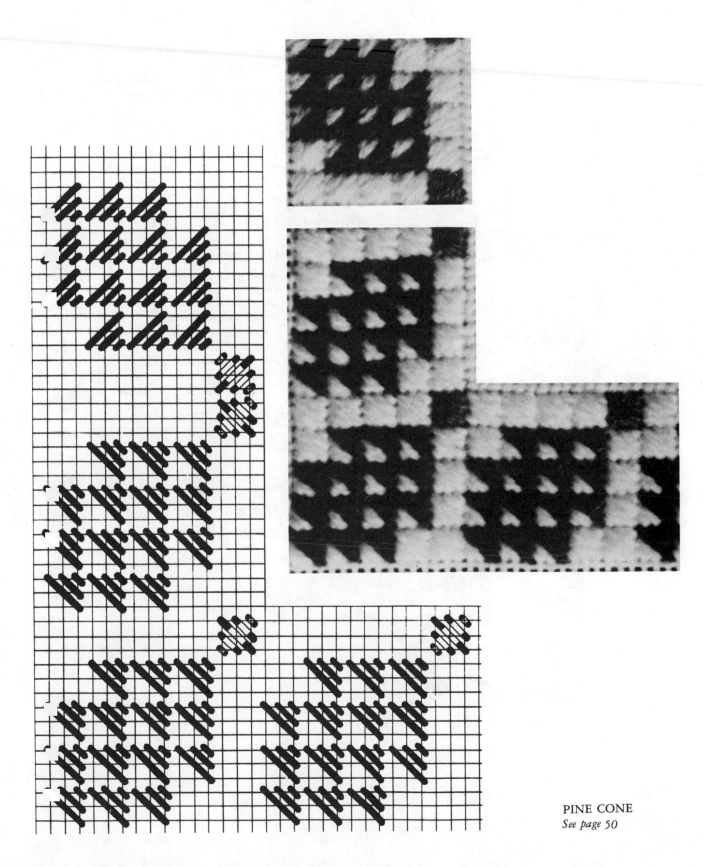

PINE CONE
See page 50

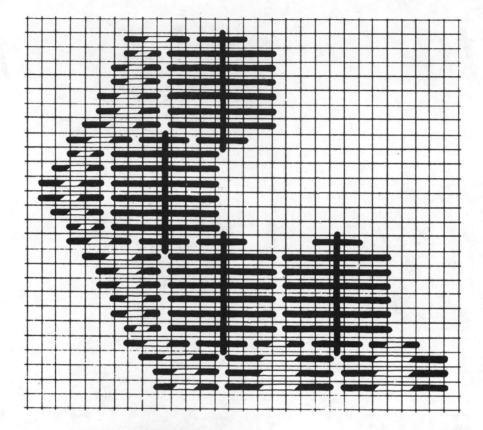

RAINBOW
TILES
See page 44

Stitch Directions

Stitching Guide

We have used Appleton crewel yarn to stitch the samples in this book. The number of strands of yarn listed for Appleton and for Persian yarn will usually cover #14 canvas properly. Some yarns may vary in thickness; adjust the number of strands used as necessary to cover the canvas.

		APPLETON	PERSIAN
1.	Backstitch	3	2
2.	Bargello, four-step	4	3
3.	Bargello, five-step	4	3
4.	Basketweave (diagonal tent)	3	2
5.	Brick	4	3
6.	Byzantine	3	2
7.	Cashmere, continuing	3	2
8.	Chequer	3	2
9.	Continental (tent)	3	2
10.	Cross	4	3
11.	Diagonal	3	2
12.	Diamond eye	3	2
13.	Double straight cross	4	3
14.	Flat, one-direction	3	2
15.	Flat, two-direction	3	2
16.	Gobelin, upright	4	3
17.	Gobelin, encroached	4	3
18.	Hungarian	4	3
19.	Long-armed cross	3	2
20.	Long-armed cross, diagonal	2	1
21.	Long straight	4	3
22.	Milanese, diagonal	3	2
23.	Milanese, straight	4	3
24.	Mosaic	3	2
25.	Mosaic, continuing	3	2
26.	Parisian	4	3
27.	Rice	4	3
28.	Scotch	3	2
29.	Smyrna cross	5	3
30.	Woven	4	3

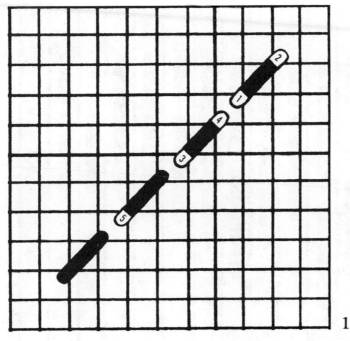

1. BACKSTITCH

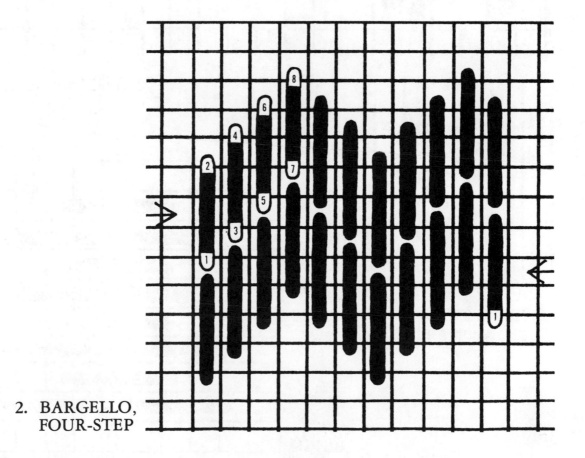

2. BARGELLO,
FOUR-STEP

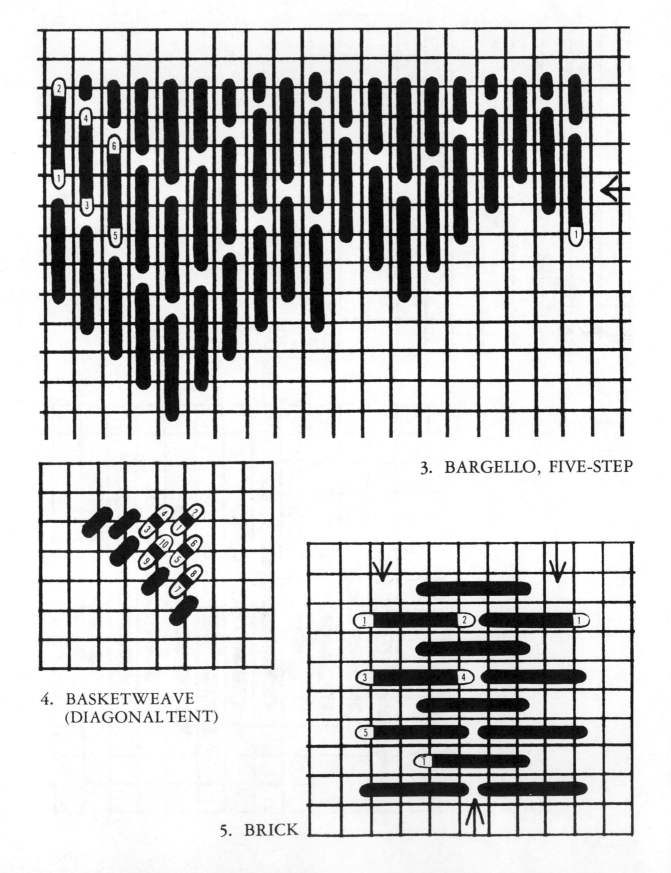

3. BARGELLO, FIVE-STEP

4. BASKETWEAVE (DIAGONAL TENT)

5. BRICK

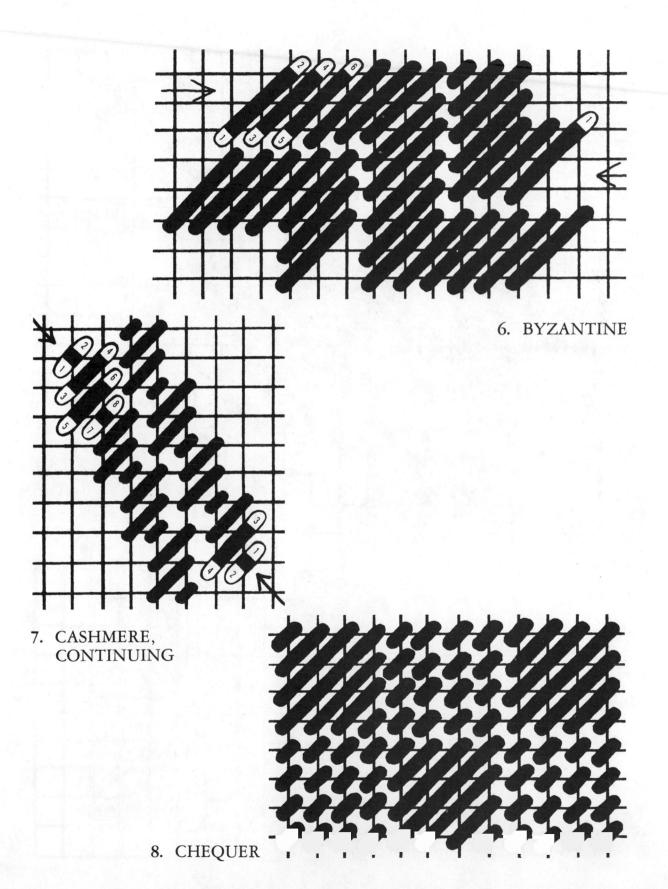

6. BYZANTINE

7. CASHMERE,
CONTINUING

8. CHEQUER

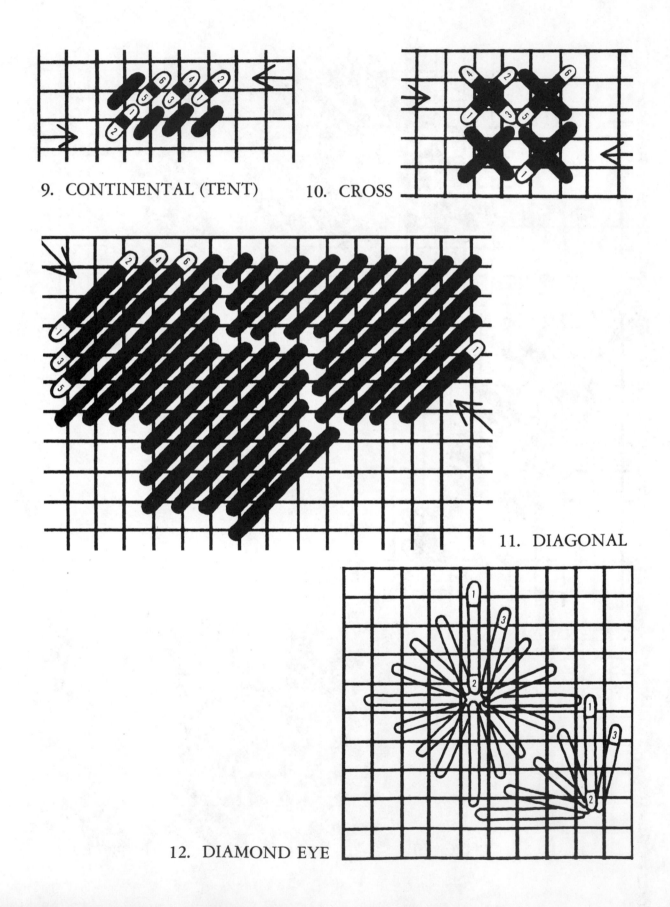

9. CONTINENTAL (TENT)

10. CROSS

11. DIAGONAL

12. DIAMOND EYE

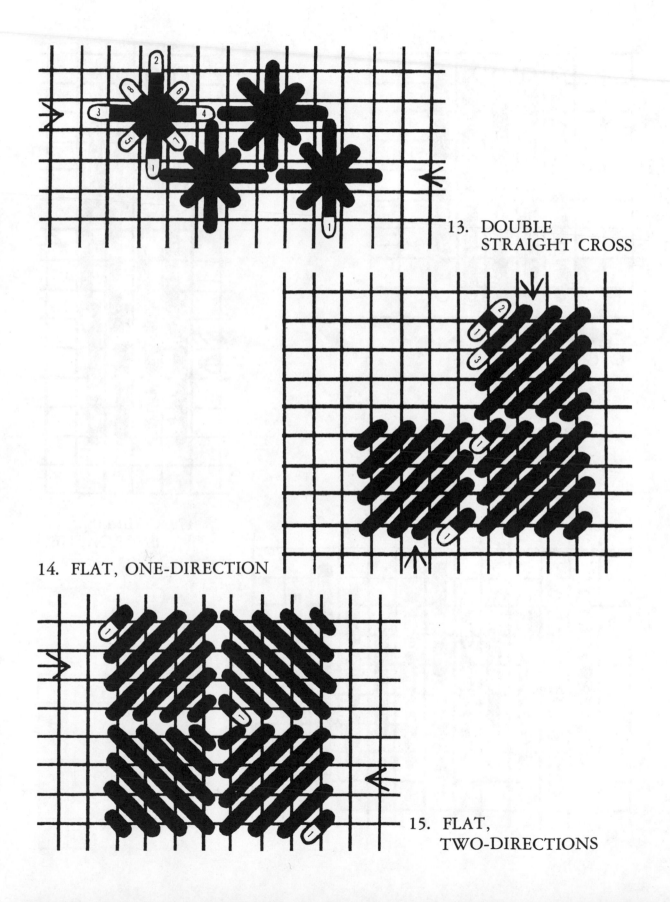

13. DOUBLE STRAIGHT CROSS

14. FLAT, ONE-DIRECTION

15. FLAT, TWO-DIRECTIONS

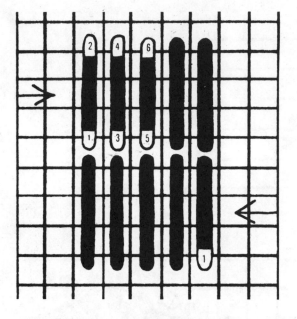

16. GOBELIN, UPRIGHT

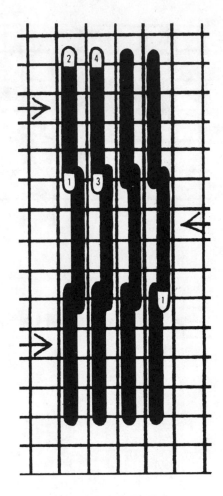

17. GOBELIN, ENCROACHED

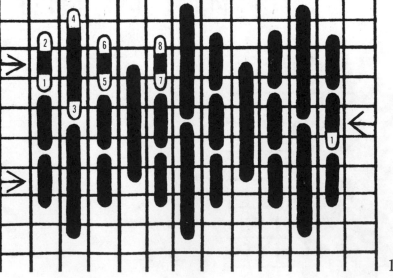

18. HUNGARIAN

19. LONG-ARMED CROSS

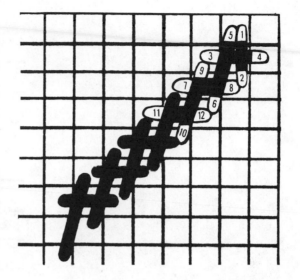

20. LONG-ARMED CROSS, DIAGONAL

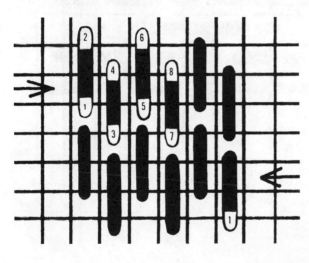

21. LONG STRAIGHT

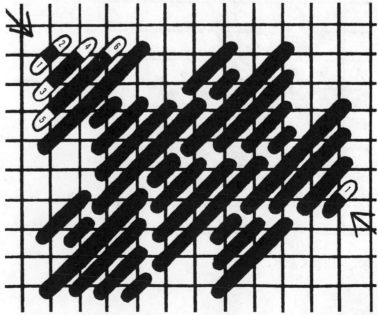

22. MILANESE, DIAGONAL

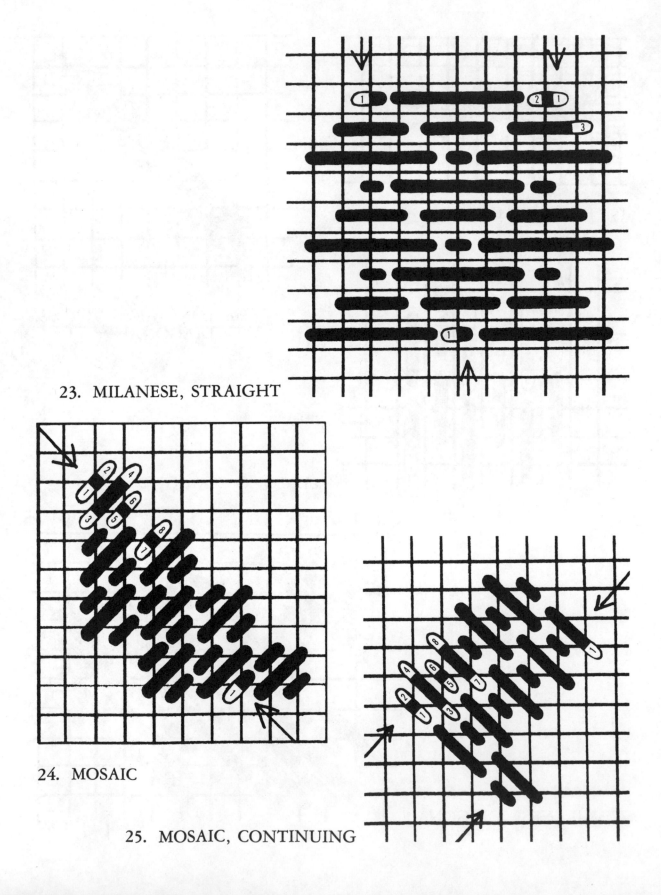

23. MILANESE, STRAIGHT

24. MOSAIC

25. MOSAIC, CONTINUING

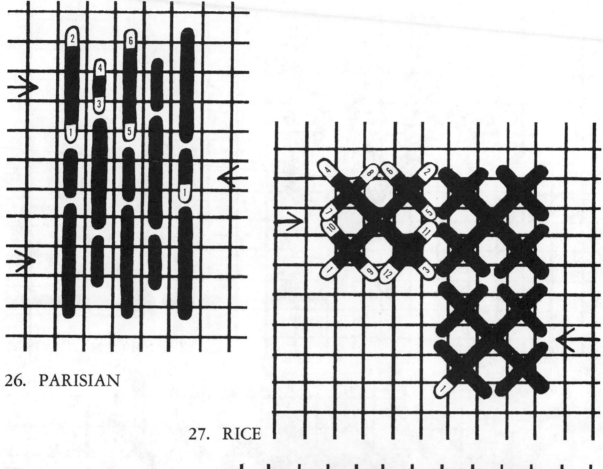

26. PARISIAN

27. RICE

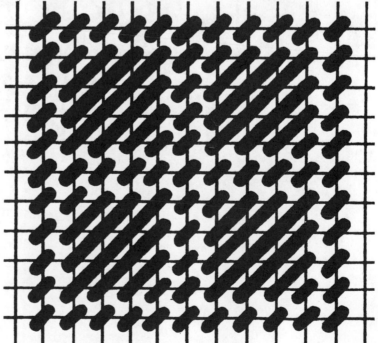

28. SCOTCH

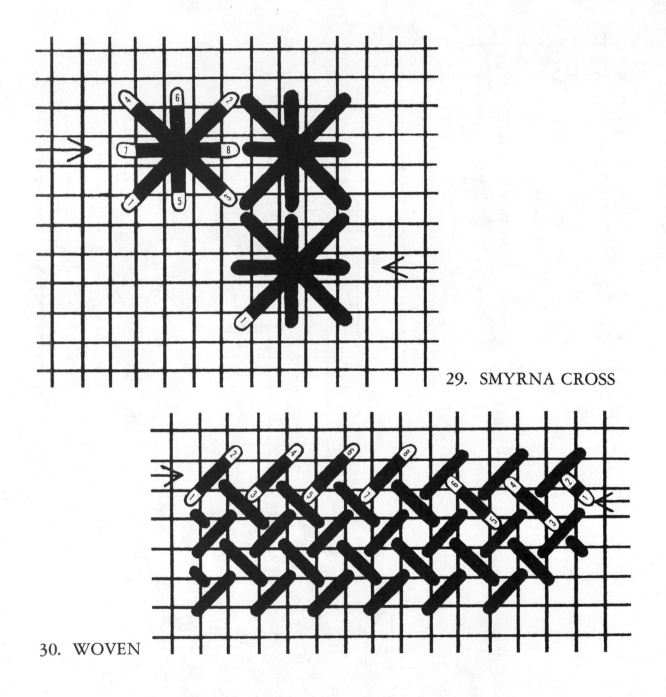

29. SMYRNA CROSS

30. WOVEN

Canvas-Needle-Yarn Chart

The designs in this book specify the canvas gauge used. That gauge indicates the type of yarn that will cover the canvas best, and the yarn used determines the number of strands per needleful. For this reason, we recommend using stranded yarn for needlepoint.

This chart is based on the amount of yarn necessary for a *diagonal* stitch.

When working with a straight stitch, 1 additional strand may be needed to cover the canvas. Because individual yarns vary slightly in thickness, it would be wise to stitch a small area on the margin of the canvas using the number of strands specified. If the canvas is not adequately covered, add another strand of yarn.

GAUGE CANVAS	YARN TYPE	AVERAGE NUMBER OF STRANDS NEEDED PER NEEDLEFUL
5	Rug Tapestry Persian	1 strand 2 strands 8 single strands
7	Rug Persian	1 strand 4 single strands
10	Tapestry Persian Crewel	1 strand 3 single strands 5 strands
12	Persian Crewel	2 single strands 4 strands
14	Persian Crewel	2 single strands 3 single strands
	Perle Cotton #3	1 strand
16/18	Persian Crewel Perle Cotton #5	1 single strand 2 strands 1 strand

The correct needle size is one that will easily hold the yarn without distorting the canvas meshes as the needle's eye passes through.

Canvas Conversion Chart. Use this chart to determine the amount of canvas needed for a design when changing the gauge of the canvas.

For example, on #14 canvas, a design measures 11". Row A is the known gauge of canvas. Row B is desired gauge. Multiply the number in the square where Row A and Row B intersect by the known dimension of the finished design. The product is the area that would be covered. If it is worked on #10 canvas, it would measure 11" × 1.4", or slightly over 15". A minimum of 1½" of unworked canvas should extend beyond the work on all four sides; it is needed for blocking and finishing.

A. KNOWN GAUGE	B. DESIRED GAUGE					
	5.0	10.0	12.0	14.0	16.0	18.0
5	1.0	0.5	0.4	0.35	0.3	0.27
10	2.0	1.0	0.8	0.7	0.6	0.5
12	2.4	1.2	1.0	0.9	0.8	0.7
14	2.8	1.4	1.2	1.0	0.9	0.8
16	3.2	1.6	1.3	1.1	1.0	0.9
18	3.6	1.8	1.5	1.3	1.1	1.0

Bibliography

Adrosko, Rita J. *Natural Dyes and Home Dyeing.* 1968. Reprint. New York: Dover Publications, 1971.

Atwater, Mary Meigs. *The Shuttlecraft Book of American Hand-Weaving.* Rev. ed. New York: Macmillan, 1966.

Betterton, Shiela. *American Textiles and Needlework.* Bath: American Museum in Britain, n.d.

————. *The American Quilt Tradition.* London: American Museum in Britain and the Commonwealth Institute, 1976.

Bishop, Robert. *New Discoveries in American Quilts.* New York: Dutton, 1975.

————, and Safanda, Elizabeth. *A Gallery of Amish Quilts: Design Diversity from a Plain People.* New York: 1976.

Burnham, H. B., and Burnham, D. K. *Keep Me Warm One Night: Early Handweaving in Eastern Canada.* Toronto: University of Toronto Press, 1973.

Channing, Marion L. *The Textile Tools of Colonial Homes.* Marion, Mass.: Marion L. Channing, 1969.

Christensen, Erwin O. *Early American Wood Carving.* 1952. Reprint. New York: Dover Publications, 1972.

Cooper, Grace R. *The Copp Family Textiles.* Washington, D.C.: Smithsonian Institution Press, 1971.

Davis, Mary Kay, and Giammattei, Helen. *Needlepoint from America's Great Quilt Designs.* New York: Workman Publishing Company, 1974.

Davis, Mildred J. *The Art of Crewel Embroidery.* New York: Crown, 1962.

Davison, Mildred. "Handwoven Coverlets in the Art Institute of Chicago." *Antiques* (May 1970), pp. 734–740.

————. "Five Related Coverlets." *Antiques* (October 1972), pp. 650–652.

————, and Mayer-Thurman, Christa C. *Coverlets.* Chicago: Art Institute of Chicago, 1973.

Emery, Irene. *The Primary Structure of Fabrics.* Washington, D.C.: Textile Museum, 1966.

Fennelly, Catherine. *Textiles in New England, 1790–1840.* Sturbridge, Mass.: Old Sturbridge Village, 1961.

Finley, Ruth E. *Old Patchwork Quilts and the Women Who Made Them.* 1929. Reprint. Newton Centre, Mass.: Charles T. Branford, 1970.

Gilbert, K. R. *Textile Machinery.* London: Science Museum, 1971.

Hall, Carrie A., and Kretsinger, Rose G. *The Romance of the Patchwork Quilt in America.* 1935. Reprint. New York: Bonanza Books, n.d.

Hall, Eliza C. *A Book of Handwoven Coverlets.* Boston: Little, Brown, 1912.

Holstein, Jonathan. *American Pieced Quilts.* Washington, D.C.: Smithsonian Institution Traveling Exhibition Service, 1972.

————. *The Pieced Quilt: An American Design Tradition.* New York: New York Graphic Society, 1973.

Hughes, Therle. *English Domestic Needlework, 1660–1860.* London: Abbey Fine Arts, n.d.

Ickis, Marguerite. *The Standard Book of Quilt Making and Collecting.* 1949. Reprint. New York: Dover Publications, 1959.

Ireys, Katharine. *The Encyclopedia of Canvas Embroidery Stitch Patterns.* New York: Thomas Y. Crowell, 1972.

Katzenberg, Dena S. *The Great American Cover-Up: Counterpanes of the Eighteenth and Nineteenth Centuries.* Baltimore: Baltimore Museum of Art, 1971.

King, Donald. *Samplers.* London: Victoria and Albert Museum, 1960.

Lipman, Jean, and Winchester, Alice. *The Flowering of American Folk Art*. New York: Viking Press in cooperation with the Whitney Museum of American Art, 1974.

McKim, Ruby Short. *One Hundred and One Patchwork Patterns*. 1931. Reprint. New York: Dover Publications, 1962.

Montgomery, Pauline. *Indiana Coverlet Weavers and Their Coverlets*. Indianapolis: Hoosier Heritage Press, 1974.

Orlovsky, Patsy, and Orlovsky, Myron. *Quilts in America*. New York: McGraw-Hill, 1974.

Peto, Florence. *American Quilts and Coverlets*. New York: Chanticleer Press, 1949.

Reinert, Guy F. "Coverlets of the Pennsylvania Germans." *Pennsylvania German Folklore Society* 13 (1948): 73.

Safford, Carleton L., and Bishop, Robert. *America's Quilts and Coverlets*. New York: Dutton, 1972.

Schetky, EthelJane McD., ed. *Dye Plants and Dyeing: A Handbook*. Brooklyn: Brooklyn Botanic Garden, 1964.

Schiffer, Margaret B. *Historical Needlework of Pennsylvania*. New York: Scribner's, 1968.

Swan, Susan Burrows. *A Winterthur Guide to American Needlework*. Wilmington, Del.: Henry Francis du Pont Winterthur Museum, 1976.

Swygert, Mrs. Luther. *Heirlooms from Old Looms*. Chicago: R. R. Donnelley, 1955.

Wardle, Patricia. *Guide to English Embroidery*. London: Victoria and Albert Museum, 1970.

White, Margaret E. *Handwoven Coverlets in the Newark Museum*. Newark: Newark Museum Association, 1947.